Hugo's Simplifie

C000017302

Portuguese Verbs
Simplified

Hugo's Language Books Limited

This edition
© 1987 Hugo's Language Books Ltd
All rights reserved
ISBN 0 85285 108 1

4th Impression 1995

Written by

Maria-Fernanda Allen

Lecturer in Portuguese at the University of Westminster
(Post-Graduate Dept. and other courses)

Set in 9/11pt English Times by
Printkings Ltd., Euston Road, London, NW1
Printed and bound in Great Britain by
Page Bros, Norwich

Contents

PART I

What is a verb? 6
   General structure

Regular and irregular verbs 11

Subject pronouns 12
   Translating 'you'
   Neuter: 'it'

Tenses 14
   Indicative tenses
   Past participle and passive tenses
   Present participle and continuous tenses
   Subjunctive tenses

Auxiliaries 25
   Translating English auxiliaries (can, do, must etc.)
   The Portuguese auxiliaries (ser, estar, ficar etc.)

Object pronouns and pronominal tenses 30
   Object pronouns
   Some irregularities
   Pronominal future and conditional

Reflexive pronouns 33

Accents and stress 36

Interrogative form 37

PART II

Model conjugations of regular verbs 40

Model conjugation of a reflexive verb 46

List of common reflexive verbs 51

PART III

Defective, impersonal and unipersonal verbs 54

Radical-changing and orthographical-changing verbs 56
Radical-changing verbs
Orthographical-changing verbs

Irregular verbs 62
Groups of verbs
Alphabetical list of conjugated irregular verbs

Verbal idioms 82

Verbs requiring prepositions 87

Index of verbs 89

Part I

What is a verb?

The verb expresses a fact (an action or state of being) and is therefore the most important part of speech. You can never speak or understand a language completely until you master the verbs. Portuguese verbs are more complicated than those in English, but this should not deter you. In this simplified method we shall endeavour to make the task as easy, clear and enjoyable as possible by avoiding obsolete or seldom-used verbs and forms, and by keeping the grammatical terminology to a minimum. Remember: *Querer é poder* - Where there's a will, there's a way.

General structure

Verbs consist of four **moods:** infinitive, indicative, subjunctive and imperative. They have two **voices:** active and passive - and in the case of Portuguese it is convenient to call the reflexive form a third 'voice'.

Portuguese is the only Romance language with two infinitives: impersonal and personal. **Impersonal infinitive** is the name of the verb, indicated in English by 'to' ('to speak') and in Portuguese by the endings *-ar, -er, -ir* and *-or,* for example: *dar, ser, abrir, pôr.*

This impersonal infinitive is also used:

(a) where English would use the present participle:

   Smoking is bad for your health
   Fumar faz mal à saude

(b) after prepositions:

   I am fed up with waiting
   Estou farta de esperar

(c) as an imperative, when the order is to nobody in particular:

Do not make any noise (= No noise!)
Não fazer barulho

(d) as a noun:

The human being
O ser humano

Sunset
O pôr do sol

The **personal infinitive,** although peculiar to the Portuguese language, need not worry you. Most students appreciate it, since it simplifies sentence structure, makes speech clearer and can replace the more dreaded subjunctive in some of its uses. As its name suggests, the personal infinitive shows the persons involved or emphasized in that infinitive, by means of its respective endings. There are only three of them to remember, being the same for either regular or irregular verbs: *-es, -mos, -em,* indicating 'you', 'us', 'them'. For example:

This book is for us to read
Este livro é para lermos

For further rules, please consult Hugo's 'Portuguese in Three Months', pages 101-2.

The **indicative** mood indicates an actual event which takes place (present tense), took place (past tense), was taking place (imperfect tense) or will take place (future tense). Besides these tenses, it also has its compound tenses and the conditional.

The **subjunctive** mood expresses a wish, a possibility ('If I were you'), something which is not an actual fact ('that I may/might'). It has practically disappeared in English but it is very much in use in Portuguese. It is used in a dependent clause, usually introduced by *que* ('that').

The subjunctive mood has almost as many tenses as the indicative:

Present: *Espero que fale inglês*
I hope you speak English

Imperfect: *Disse-lhe que viesse cedo*
I told him to come early

Perfect: *Lamento que tenha estado doente*
I am sorry you have been ill

Pluperfect: *Se me tivesse telefonado...*
If you had rung me...

These last two tenses are compound (that is, they are formed from more than one word) and are formed with the aid of the verb *ter* ('to have') and the past participle of the main verb - as they would be in English. The subjunctive also boasts a future and a compound future (or future perfect):

Future: *Quando eu for a Portugal...*
When I (shall) go to Portugal...

Future
perfect: *Sairei quando tiver feito este trabalho*
I shall go out when I (shall) have finished this work

What distinguishes the subjunctive from the indicative mood is that these sentences are all dependent on a main clause such as 'I hope', 'I told him' (an order), 'I am sorry' and 'If': that is, the action is hypothetical. In the indicative present the first sentence, for example, would read *Fala inglês* - You speak English. The subjunctive mood, which is comprehensively explained in our 'Portuguese in Three Months', is very much alive in all Portuguese-speaking countries.

The **imperative** mood expresses a command, and it has only two persons: the singular and the plural 'you', *tu* and *vós*. The *vós* form is almost obsolete; to replace this person in modern Portuguese, as well as other persons lacking in the true imperative, the present subjunctive is used for a polite order and a negative command (these forms are shown in brackets in our verb conjugations and lists of verbs).

Familiar 'you', singular, with the imperative:

Fala depressa
Speak quickly

Familiar 'you', singular, with the subjunctive (negative):

Não fales em inglês
Do not speak in English

Polite 'you', singular, subjunctive:

Fale devagar
Speak slowly

'You', plural, subjunctive:

Falem mais alto
Speak louder

'You' ('Ye'), plural, imperative:

Falai de Deus
Speak of God

'We', subjunctive:

Falemos em português
Let us speak in Portuguese

When a verb is described as being in the **active** voice, the subject of that verb is the doer of the action expressed ('the boy is crying'); this voice often expresses a state or condition ('the river flows'). The tenses of the active voice are described in the section on 'Tenses' below.

In the **passive** voice the subject receives the action expressed ('the boy was smacked'). The formation of the passive follows the same pattern in Portuguese as in English; we take the auxiliary *ser* ('to be') followed by the past participle of the main verb.

Active: *Conto uma história*
            I tell a story

Passive: *Uma história é contada por mim*
             A story is told by me

A **reflexive** verb is one that in English is followed by one of the reflexive pronouns: 'myself', 'himself', etc. For example, 'I am warming the room' is not reflexive, while 'I am warming myself' is.

In Portuguese reflexive verbs are immediately recognizable by the hyphen and *se* ('oneself') after the infinitive: *sentar-se* 'to sit'. In a sentence, this *se* is replaced by the other reflexive pronouns, according to the subject: *eu sento-me* 'I sit'. Several of these verbs also exist in a non-reflexive form, without the *se,* in many instances with a different meaning:

pôr to put, place	*pôr-se a* to begin to
rir to laugh	*rir-se de* to make fun of, to laugh at

Regular and irregular verbs

Verbs are either regular or irregular. **Regular** verbs are those which follow the model conjugations shown in Part II; their stems do not alter. (The stem is the part of the verb preceding the ending.) These verbs are divided into three groups or conjugations, the infinitives of which end in -*ar* (*falar*, 1st conjugation), -*er* (*comer*, 2nd conjugation) and -*ir* (*abrir*, 3rd conjugation). Once you have studied the table of model verbs in Part II you will be able to conjugate any regular verb in any tense.

Irregular verbs are those which do not conform. Their stems change depending on the subject (person), number (singular or plural) and tense (present, past, etc.). Some of these verbs have some similarities and will therefore be grouped together where possible in the lists in Part III. The verb *pôr* stands in a class of its own, together with its compounds. There are also some verbs which are not strictly irregular, but which contain some irregularities: these include the radical-changing and orthographical-changing (or spelling-changing) verbs, which are also listed in Part III.

A few verbs lack some of the usual persons or tenses. These are the defective, impersonal and unipersonal verbs. They are also covered in Part III.

Subject pronouns

Here is a list of the Portuguese subject pronouns:

Singular	Plural
eu I (1st person)	*nós* we (1st person)
tu you (2nd person, familiar)	*vós* you (2nd person, obsolete)
você you (2nd person, informal)	*vocês* you (2nd person, familiar and informal)
o senhor you (2nd person, male, formal)	*os senhores* you (2nd person, male or mixed, formal)
a senhora you (2nd person, female, formal)	*as senhoras* you (2nd person, female, formal)
ele he, it (3rd person)	*eles* they (3rd person, male)
ela she, it (3rd person)	*elas* they (3rd person, female)

Translating 'you'

As you see, Portuguese has several translations for the English 'you'. *Tu* is very familiar and is reserved for close friends, lovers and children. *Você* - the most popular form of address in Brazil - is used in Portugal among casual acquaintances, colleagues, etc., implying a certain degree of equality in age and status. A married person would address a single one (if not older) with *você*, but not the other way round; the same goes for employer/employee and teacher/student relationships. *Você* can be considered rude if used to address the wrong person. It is a shortened form of *vossemecê*, which is still popular among provincial old folk and originated in the respectful form of address *Vossa Mercê*.

In a formal context, say *a senhora* when addressing a lady, especially a married one, and *o senhor* for a man. Use *os senhores* to address men or a mixed group and *as senhoras* for women. Although they mean 'you', *você*, *o senhor* and *a senhora* use the third person singular form of the verb, the same as for 'he' or 'she'; *vocês*, *os senhores* and *as senhoras* use the third person verbal form in the plural, the same as for 'they'.

Vós is practically obsolete, although it is found in classical literature. For this reason, this form will appear in brackets in our lists of verb forms.

In conversation the subject pronouns *eu, tu, nós* (and *vós*) can usually be omitted since the verb form on its own is sufficient to indicate the subject. For example:

Falas português?
Do you speak Portuguese? (familiar)

Falamos português
We speak Portuguese

Neuter: 'it'

There is no neuter in the Portuguese language except in the forms *isto* (this), *isso* (that) and *aquilo* (that - of something further away). All Portuguese nouns have either masculine or feminine gender, and as the subject of a sentence the word 'it' is translated by either *ele* (he) or *ela* (she) depending on the gender of the thing in question. (See the table of pronouns at the beginning of this section.)

As the object of a sentence, 'it' is often omitted:

Gosta de vinho? Sim, gosto.
Do you like wine? Yes, I like (it).

Tenses (tempos)

Indicative tenses (indicativo)

Present   A present tense form such as *falo* translates not only the English present tense ('I speak') but also the progressive form ('I am speaking'), and in some contexts the future ('I shall speak') and even the perfect ('I have spoken') when the sentence contains *há* and relates to a period of time.

> *Como carne*
> I eat meat/I am eating meat/I do eat meat

> *Amanhã como carne*
> Tomorrow I shall eat meat

> *Há dois meses que não como carne*
> I haven't eaten meat for two months

To form the present tense you add the following endings to the stems of the regular verbs:

(1st conjugation) verbs ending in *-ar: -o, -as, -a, -amos (-ais,) -am*
(2nd conjugation) verbs ending in *-er: -o, -es, -e, -emos, (-eis,) -em*
(3rd conjugation) verbs ending in *-ir: -o, -es, -e, -imos, (-is,) -em*

Make it easy on yourself! If you ignore the classical *vós* form in brackets and the familiar *tu*, you are left with only four lines to commit to memory. Note that all the first persons ('I'. forms) end in *-o.* This holds true for irregular verbs too, with six exceptions:

sou (I am), *estou* (I am), *dou* (I give), *vou* (I go), *sei* (I know), *hei* (I have – and other meanings, covered below).

The first person plural ('we') always ends in *-mos,* in any tense and any verb, regular or irregular. A second or third person plural ('you' or 'they') is immediately recognizable by its ending *-em* or *-am,* with the exception of five verbs in the present tense:

são, estão ('you/they are'), *vão* ('they go'), *dão* ('they give'), *hão* (they have etc.)

As you will see, these endings are actually the same as the regular future tense ending.

Past definite   This tense (also known as the simple preterite) has a greater tendency to be irregular than any other. It corresponds to several English forms: for example, *falei* can be translated 'I spoke', 'I did speak', 'I have spoken'.

Ontem comi muito
Yesterday I ate a lot

Já comi, obrigado
I have already eaten, thank you

Não bebi nada
I did not drink anything

The following endings are added to the stem of the infinitive:

(1st conjugation) verbs in *-ar: -ei, -aste, -ou, -ámos, (-astes,) -aram*
(2nd conjugation) verbs in *-er: -i, -este, -eu, -emos, (-estes,) -eram*
(3rd conjugation) verbs in *-ir: -i, -iste, -iu, -imos, (-istes,) -iram*

Imperfect   This, the easiest tense to form, is not always the easiest for the English to understand. As its name suggests, it refers to less definite or complete actions than the other past tense. It can refer to past actions which were habitual or incomplete, which were interrupted or taking place at the same time as another action; it is also sometimes used in descriptive sequences. The equivalent of *falava*, for example, can be 'I was speaking', 'I used to speak', 'I spoke'.

Falava com a tua mãe quando ele entrou
I was talking to your mother when he came in

Ela ia sempre à praia
She always went to the beach

Estava muito calor
It was very hot

This tense has only two sets of endings for all verbs, regular and irregular:

verbs in *-ar: -ava, -avas, -ava, -ávamos, (-áveis,) -avam*
verbs in *-er* and *-ir: -ia, -ias, -ia, -íamos, (-íeis,) -iam*

There are four exceptions:

pôr: punha, punhas, punha, púnhamos, (púnheis), punham
ser: era, eras, era, éramos, (éreis,) eram
ter: tinha, tinhas, tinha, tínhamos, (tínheis,) tinham
vir: vinha, vinhas, vinha, vínhamos, (vínheis,) vinham

Note that the imperfect is often used in place of the conditional, especially in the case of the verbs *querer* ('to want') and *gostar* ('to like').

Perfect   The perfect tense expresses an action started in the past and continuing almost up to the present; it is formed with the present indicative of the auxiliary verb *ter* (or less commonly *haver*) and the past participle of the main verb.

Tenho falado muito
I have been speaking a lot (NOT I have spoken)

Remember that the English 'I have spoken' or the French 'j'ai parlé' are translated in Portuguese by *falei* (past definite).

Pluperfect: simple and compound   The simple pluperfect, which is not used in speech, is formed by adding *-a* to the infinitive of regular verbs: *(falar - falara, vender - vendera)* and by removing the *m* from the third person plural of the past definite for irregular verbs *(fizeram - fizera, vieram - viera, foram - fora, trouxeram - trouxera)*.

In speech this tense is replaced by the compound pluperfect, which uses the imperfect indicative of the auxiliary verb *ter* plus the past participle of the main verb in question. (All the compound tenses can also - less commonly - be formed with *haver.*)

The pluperfect, simple or compound, expresses an action which took place in the past prior to another past action - as does the English pluperfect.

Quando eu cheguei já ele tinha partido
When I arrived he had already left

Future: simple and compound   The Portuguese simple future translates the English future, and the compound future (or future perfect) translates the English future perfect. The simple future is very simple to form, since it has only one set of endings for all verbs: *-ei, -ás, -á, -emos, (-eis,) -ão.* These endings are added to the infinitive, except in the case of three verbs:

dizer: direi, dirás, dirá, diremos, (direis,) dirão
fazer: farei, farás, fará, faremos, (fareis,) farão
trazer: trarei, trarás, trará, traremos, (trareis,) trarão

Falarei contigo amanhã
I shall speak to you tomorrow

Ele fará o possível
He will do his best

Remember that futurity can also be expressed by the present tense, as described above.

The compound future or future perfect is formed with the future of the auxiliary *ter* and the past participle of the main verb.

Por essa altura já eu terei acabado tudo
By then I shall have finished everything

Conditional: simple and compound   The simple conditional corresponds to the English conditional tense and is also easy to form; you add the following endings to the infinitive: *-ia, -ias, -ia, -íamos, (-íeis,) -iam.* As in the future tense, the same three verbs are exceptions to this rule:

dizer: diria, dirias, diria, diríamos, (diríeis,) diriam
fazer: faria, farias, faria, faríamos, (faríeis,) fariam
trazer: traria, trarias, traria, traríamos, (traríeis,) trariam

Gostaria muito de ir a Portugal
I should very much like to go to Portugal

The compound conditional or conditional perfect also corresponds to the English conditional perfect and is again formed as in English, with the auxiliary *ter* in the conditional tense followed by the past participle of the main verb.

Ele não se teria engasgado se não tivesse bebido tão depressa
He would not have choked (himself) if he had not drunk so fast

In this example *teria engasgado* is the conditional perfect form and *tivesse bebido* is a subjunctive form.

Past participle and passive tenses

As you have seen, the past participle is used in the active voice to form the compound tenses, with the help of the auxiliary verb *ter* (and less commonly with *haver*). It is also used to form the passive tenses with the auxiliary *ser;* these tenses are less used in Portuguese than in English.

Present passive:	*Ela é amada por todos* She is loved by everybody
Past definite passive:	*A carta foi escrita pela irmã* The letter was written by his/her sister

With the auxiliary *estar,* the past participle is used in descriptive sentences, where it doubles as an adjective:

Nós estamos cansados
We are tired

Any past participle which follows *ser* or *estar* will agree in gender and number with the subject, as seen in the examples.

The past participle is formed by adding the following endings to the stems of verbs, whether regular or irregular:

-*ar* verbs: -*ado* (*falado* spoken)
-*er* verbs: -*ido* (*tido* had, *sido* been)
-*ir* verbs: -*ido* (*partido* left, *ido* gone)

Irregular past participles Some verbs, although otherwise regular, have irregular past participles. Here is a list of irregular past participles:

abrir *(to open)*	aberto
cobrir *(to cover)*	coberto
dizer *(to tell)*	dito
escrever *(to write)*	escrito
fazer *(to do/make)*	feito
ganhar *(to earn/win)*	ganho
gastar *(to spend)*	gasto
pagar *(to pay)*	pago
pôr *(to put/place)*	posto
ver *(to see)*	visto
vir *(to come)*	vindo

Some verbs have two past participles: a regular one, which is invariable and is conjugated with the auxiliaries *ter* and occasionally *haver,* and an irregular past participle which must agree in gender and number with the subject and follows *ser* or *estar.* The latter also doubles as an adjective. A list of these verbs follows:

aceitar *(to accept)*	aceitado	aceito/aceite
acender *(to switch on)*	acendido	aceso
afligir *(to afflict/worry)*	afligido	aflito
agradecer *(to thank)*	agradecido	grato
anexar *(to annex)*	anexado	anexo
benzer *(to bless)*	benzido	bento
cativar *(to captivate)*	cativado	cativo
cegar *(to blind)*	cegado	cego
completar *(to complete)*	completado	completo
concluir *(to conclude)*	concluído	concluso

confundir *(to confound)*	confundido	confuso
convencer *(to convince)*	convencido	convicto
corromper *(to corrupt)*	corrompido	corrupto
defender *(to defend)*	defendido	defeso
descalçar *(to take off (shoes))*	descalçado	descalço
desertar *(to desert)*	desertado	deserto
eleger *(to elect)*	elegido	eleito
entregar *(to hand in)*	entregado	entregue
envolver *(to wrap/involve)*	envolvida	envolto
enxugar *(to dry)*	enxugado	enxuto
erigir *(to erect)*	erigido	erecto
exprimir *(to express)*	exprimido	expresso
expulsar *(to expel)*	expulsado	expulso
extinguir *(to extinguish)*	extinguido	extinto
extrair *(to extract)*	extraído	extracto
falsificar *(to falsify)*	falsificado	falso
fartar *(to have enough)*	fartado	farto
fixar *(to fix)*	fixado	fixo
frigir *(to fry)*	frigido	frito
fritar *(to fry)*	fritado	frito
imprimir *(to print)*	imprimido	impresso
incluir *(to include)*	incluído	incluso
infectar *(to infect)*	infectado	infecto
inquietar *(to disturb/worry)*	inquietado	inquieto
inserir *(to insert)*	inserido	inserto
inverter *(to invert/reverse)*	invertido	inverso
isentar *(to exempt)*	isentado	isento
juntar *(to join)*	juntado	junto
libertar *(to free)*	libertado	liberto
limpar *(to clean)*	limpado	limpo
manifestar *(to manifest)*	manifestado	manifesto
matar *(to kill)*	matado	morto
morrer *(to die)*	morrido	morto
murchar *(to wilt/wither)*	murchado	murcho
ocultar *(to hide)*	ocultado	oculto
oprimir *(to oppress)*	oprimido	opresso
perverter *(to pervert)*	pervertido	perverso

prender *(to arrest)*	prendido	preso
professar *(to profess)*	professado	professo
repelir *(to repel)*	repelido	repulso
restringir *(to restrain)*	restringido	restrito
revolver *(to revolve)*	revolvido	revolto
romper *(to break/tear)*	rompido	roto
salvar *(to save)*	salvado	salvo
secar *(to dry)*	secado	seco
segurar *(to hold)*	segurado	seguro
soltar *(to loosen)*	soltado	solto
submergir *(to submerge)*	submergido	submerso
submeter *(to submit)*	submetido	submisso
sujeitar *(to subdue/subject)*	sujeitado	sujeito
suspeitar *(to suspect)*	suspeitado	suspeito
suspender *(to suspend)*	suspendido	suspenso
tingir *(to dye/tinge)*	tingido	tinto

Present participle and continuous tenses

The present participle, which in English ends in 'ing', is formed in Portuguese by removing the final *r* from the infinitive and adding *-ndo*:

falar - *falando* speaking
ver - *vendo* seeing
partir - *partindo* leaving
pôr - *pondo* putting

The Portuguese present participle is less used than the English, since the English continuous tenses ('I am speaking', etc.) are translated either by a simple tense or by the verb *estar a* plus the infinitive of the main verb. For example, the present continuous 'I am speaking' is rendered by the present tense *falo* or by *estou a falar*. Note that in Brazil, however, exactly the same form is used as in English: *estou falando*.

There are other continuous tenses, all of which use the verb *estar a* in the appropriate tense plus the infinitive of the main verb:

Estava a falar
I was speaking (= in the very act of speaking)

Estarei a falar amanhã
I shall be speaking tomorrow

As in English, the present participle can be used in a subordinate clause to express continuity of action or actions by the same subject. It can start a sentence.

Falando de férias, onde foi no verão passado?
Speaking of holidays, where did you go last summer?

Diverti-me na festa comendo, bebendo e dançando
I enjoyed myself at the party eating, drinking and dancing

Subjunctive tenses

The subjunctive mood (called *conjuntivo* in Portugal and *subjuntivo* in Brazil) was introduced in the section 'What is a verb? General structure' above. It has almost as many tenses as the indicative mood and is in full use in all Portuguese-speaking countries.

Present　The present subjunctive has the following endings, which are added to the stems of the regular verbs:

(1st conjugation) verbs in *-ar:* -e, -es, -e, -emos, (-eis,) -em
(2nd conjugation) verbs in *-er:* -a, -as, -a, -amos, (-ais,) -am
(3rd conjugation) verbs in *-ir:* -a, -as, -a, -amos, (-ais,) -am

With the irregular verbs you must remember the first person of the present indicative (e.g. *tenho)* and change its last *o* to *a* (e.g. *tenha).* The other endings follow:

eu tenha, tu tenhas, ele tenha, nós tenhamos, (vós tenhais,) eles tenham

There are only seven exceptions to this golden rule:

dar (to give)　　　*dou* (I give)　　　*dê, dês, dê,* etc.

estar (to be)	*estou* (I am)	*esteja* (that I may be, etc.)
haver (to have)	*hei*	*haja*
ir (to go)	*vou*	*vá*
querer (to want)	*quero*	*queira*
saber (to know)	*sei*	*saiba*
ser (to be)	*sou*	*seja*

Imperfect The imperfect subjunctive of the regular verbs has the following endings, added to the stem:

(1st conj.) verbs in *-ar: -asse, -asses, -asse, -ássemos, (-ásseis), -assem*
(2nd conj.) verbs in *-er: -esse, -esses, -esse, -êssemos, (-êsseis,) -essem*
(3rd conj.) verbs in *-ir: -isse, -isses, -isse, -íssemos, (-ísseis,) -issem*

For the irregular verbs this tense is based on the first person form of the past definite of the indicative, adding the following endings:

-sse, -sses, -sse, -ssemos, (-sseis,) -ssem

For example: *trouxe* (I brought) becomes *trouxesse* (that I might bring). Note that in the first (and second) persons plural an accent (always the acute í) is added to the vowel preceding the ending. So you have: *trouxéssemos* (and *trouxésseis*).

There are four exceptions:

ser (to be)	*fui* (I was)	*fosse* (that I might be, etc.)
ir (to go)	*fui*	*fosse*
dar (to give)	*dei*	*desse*
vir (to come)	*vim*	*viesse*

Did you notice that the verbs *ser* and *ir* have the same past definite and consequently the same imperfect subjunctive?

Future The same rules for the irregular verbs also apply to the future subjunctive, only this time you add the following endings to that past definite:

-r, -res, -r, -rmos, (-rdes,) -rem

Thus *trouxe* (I brought) becomes *trouxer* (if/when I shall bring). The four verbs shown above as irregular in the imperfect are also exceptions here: *ser/ir - for, dar - der, vir - vier.*

As for the regular verbs, you add *-ar, er* or *-ir* to the stem for the first person: in other words, you leave the infinitive as it is. Here are the endings:

(1st conj.) verbs in *-ar: -ar, -ares, -ar, -armos, (-ardes,) -arem*
(2nd conj.) verbs in *-er: -er, -eres, -er, -ermos, (-erdes,) -erem*
(3rd conj.) verbs in *-ir: -ir, -ires, -ir, -irmos, (-irdes,) -irem*

Incidentally, this tense is formed in exactly the same way as the personal infinitive of the regular verbs:

se nós falarmos (future subjunctive)
if we speak

ao falarmos (personal infinitive)
on (our) speaking

Auxiliaries

Auxiliaries are verbs which are used in combination with other verbs to form the compound tenses, as described in the section on 'Tenses' above, or to express probability, obligation, etc. Some examples of English auxiliaries are 'must', 'shall', 'ought'. In the paragraphs below we give you some guidelines on how to translate the English auxiliaries into Portuguese, and some notes on the use of the Portuguese auxiliaries.

Translating English auxiliaries

Can and **could,** meaning 'to be able to' or 'to be allowed to', are translated by the verb *poder,* with its past definite *pude* or even more frequently its imperfect *podia* translating 'could':

Podes ir   *Não pude ir*
You can go   I could not go

Podia abrir a janela?
Could you open the window?

When 'can' refers to knowledge, as in 'Can you speak English?', the verb *saber* is used:

Eu sei falar francês
I can (= I know how to) speak French

Sabe nadar?
Can you swim?

Ought to, should and sometimes **must** - i.e. obligation - are best translated by *dever,* in the present and imperfect indicative and subjunctive, and sometimes in the conditional.

Eu devia trabalhar mais (imperfect)
I should work more

Devemos respeitar as pessoas mais velhas (present)
We must/ought to respect older people

Am to, are to, etc. also correspond to *dever*:

Você deve telefonar-me para o escritório
You are to ring me at the office

'Ought to' or 'should' can also, though less frequently, be rendered by *haver de* in the imperfect tense:

Ele havia de me dizer
He should have told me

Remember that 'should' in the sense of 'would', however, is a conditional (for example, 'I should like to...') and is translated by the conditional tense: see the section on 'Tenses' above.

Must or **have to** - i.e. compulsion - are translated by *ter de* or *ter que* plus the infinitive of the main verb:

Tenho que trabalhar amanhã
I have to work tomorrow

Ele teve de trabalhar ontem
He had to work yesterday

Do, did, don't and **didn't** have no equivalent auxiliary in Portuguese. In most questions ('Do you...? Did he...?') the word order is the same as in the affirmative; the only change is in the inflexion. To form a negative ('I don't..., He didn't...') you simply place *não* ('no/not') before the verb.

Ele fala inglês?
Does he speak English?

Não quer vir? Sim, quero
Don't you want to come? Yes, I do

Não falo francês
I do not speak French

Shall and **will** are of course used to form the future tense in English, so in sentences like 'I shall go to Brazil' and 'he will come with me' they are simply translated by the Portuguese future tense (see the section on 'Tenses' above). But when used to imply a firm intention or strong obligation, as in 'I WILL go to Brazil and he SHALL come with me', they are rendered by the auxiliary *haver de* in the present tense, followed by the infinitive of the main verb: *hei-de ir ao Brasil e ele há-de vir comigo.*

Portuguese auxiliaries

Ser and **estar** (both meaning 'to be') are used both as auxiliaries and as verbs in their own right. As an auxiliary, *ser* is used to form the passive voice, as described in the first section 'What is a verb? General structure' above. *Estar* is used as an auxiliary to form the continuous tenses, followed by *a* and an infinitive (in Portugal) or by a present participle (in Brazil), as described in the section on 'Tenses: Present participle and continuous tenses' above. In their capacity as verbs in their own right, *ser* and *estar* are described here. (You will also find some idiomatic expressions with *ser* and *estar* in Part III.)

Ser is what you are, who you are, what you are called - even if this is not on a permanent basis. It denotes inherent characteristics, one's profession or calling and status.

Sou portuguesa	*Sou alta*	*Sou um turista*
I am Portuguese	I am tall	I am a tourist
Sou aluno	*Sou solteiro*	
I am a pupil	I am single	

When a student is told that *ser* describes permanent situations, he or she may make mistakes regarding some of the examples given above. In the case of 'when I was a child', for example, the English student quite rightly considers this a passing phase and uses the temporary verb *estar*. But *ser* should be used: you were CALLED a child, you had that identity at that time.

Ser also denotes origin or possession:

> *Ela é de Londres*
> She is from London
>
> *Este lápis é meu*
> This pencil is mine
>
> *Esta casa é do senhor Silva*
> This house is Mr Silva's

(Note that in sentences expressing possession you use *de* (of - *de* + *o* = *do*) unless you have a possessive pronoun such as *meu*.)

Finally, *ser* is used in some impersonal sentences, in telling the time and in talking about well-known places and buildings. Here are some examples:

> *É preciso*
> It is necessary
>
> *É meio-dia*
> It is noon
>
> *Onde é o Rossio?*
> Where is Rossio (Square)?

Estar denotes a temporary action, location, situation or feeling:

> *Está calor*
> It is hot
>
> *Ela está linda*
> She is looking beautiful
>
> *Onde está a minha chave?*
> Where is my key?
>
> *Estou doente*
> I am sick

Andar ('to walk/to move/to be') is the verb which expresses movement through space or time. It can be used optionally in place of *estar*, especially in the continuous tenses (see 'Tenses' above) and in sentences expressing continuing states:

> *Ando a fazer um vestido*
> I am making a dress
>
> *Ela anda grávida*
> She is pregnant
>
> *Ando muito cansada*
> I am/I have been feeling very tired

Although *estar* and *andar* can be used interchangeably in most sentences, at times there is a subtle difference which leads a Portuguese person to prefer to use one to the other. In the sentence *ando cansada* the implication is that the person has been tired up to and including the present moment; if I chose to say *estou cansada,* it would mean that I was tired NOW.

Andar is used in the following expressions to describe modes of travel:

andar de carro to go by car
andar de bicicleta to ride a bicycle
andar a cavalo to ride a horse
andar a pé to walk

Ficar ('to stay/to remain/to be') is sometimes used in preference to *estar,* for example when you want to say that someone is sad, happy, etc. as a result of some news:

Fico contente de saber que vens
I am glad to know you are coming

Fiquei a saber que...
I came to know that...

Fico à espera do teu telefonema
I shall await (= remain waiting for) your call

Acabar means 'to finish', but *acabar de* plus an infinitive means 'to have just...'. For example:

Acabo de ler um livro muito bom
I have just read a very good book

Voltar means 'to turn/to return', but *voltar a* plus an infinitive means 'to (do something) again'. The same goes for **tornar** ('to turn'):

Não volte a fazer isso   *Ele tornou a bater nela*
Don't do that again   He has struck her again

Ter and occasionally **haver**, you will remember, are used in the formation of the compound tenses (see the section on 'Tenses') as well as being used to express obligation or compulsion, as described above. See also 'Verbal idioms' in Part III.

Object pronouns and pronominal tenses

Object pronouns

Direct
me me
te you (sing., familiar)

o him, it, you (m. sing., formal/
informal)
a her, it, you (f. sing., formal/
informal)
nos us
vos you (pl., obsolete)
os them, you (m. pl., formal/
informal)
as them, you (f. pl., formal/
informal)

Indirect
me (to/for) me
te (to/for) you (sing.,
familiar)
lhe (to/for) him, her, you (m.
& f. sing., formal/informal)

nos (to/for) us
vos (to/for) you (pl., obsolete)
lhes (to/for) them, you (m. &
f. pl., formal/informal)

Eu dou-o com muito prazer
I give it with great pleasure

Eu dou-lhe um conselho
I give you/him/her some advice

When direct and indirect object pronouns are used in combination, the following contracted forms arise (the indirect pronouns always precede the direct):

mo, ma it (m. & f.) to me
mos, mas them (m. & f.) to me
to, ta it (m. & f.) to you (sing., familiar)
tos, tas them to you (sing., familiar)
lho, lha it to him/her/you (sing. & pl., formal/informal)/them

no-lo, no-la it (m. & f.) to us
no-los, no-las them (m. & f.) to us
vo-lo, vo-la it to you (pl., obsolete)
vo-los, vo-las them to you (pl., obsolete)
lhos, lhas them to him/her/you (sing. & pl., formal/informal)/them

Já lhe deu a maçã? Sim, já lha dei.
Have you given him the apple? Yes, I have given it to him

The forms *no-lo, vo-lo,* etc., although common in print, are not used in conversation. Instead, only one pronoun or a disjunctive form is used:

Ele dá-nos a maçã	*Ele dá-a a nós*
He gives us the apple	He gives it to us

Note that the *lh-* remains the same in all combinations, whether the person referred to is him, her, you or them: it is only the object (i.e. the direct object) whose number and gender are shown. Since the *lh-* combinations can refer to several persons and it may not be clear who is referred to, it is better to use only one pronoun.

Some irregularities

When the verb form ends in *r, s* or *z* and is followed by one of the direct objects *o, a, os* or *as,* the above letters are omitted; *l* is added to the beginning of the object pronouns, which are linked to the verb by a hyphen:

Quero dá-lo (dar + o)
I want to give it

Nós vemo-los todos os dias (vemos + os)
We see them every day

Ela fê-lo muito bem (fez + o)
She did it very well

Note the acute accent which is added to the *a (á)* and the circumflex which is added to the *e (ê)* to replace the sound which is lost with the removal of *r, s* or *z.*

When the direct object pronouns *o, a, os* or *as* come immediately after a verb form ending in *m, ão* or *õe,* the letter *n* is added to the beginning of the pronoun to give the forms *no, na, nos* and *nas,* which are then joined to the verb by a hyphen:

Eles dão-nas (dão + as)
They give them (feminine objects)

Elas vêem-no sempre (vêem + o)
They always see him

Ela põe-na no bolso (põe + a)
She puts it (feminine object) in her pocket

Pronominal future and conditional

When the future and conditional tenses are followed by an object pronoun, the pronoun is inserted between the *r* of the verb and the respective ending. For example:

Falar-lhe-ei (falarei + lhe)
I shall speak to him/her

The pronouns follow the same rules as given above regarding the addition of the *l:*

Eu dá-lo-ei amanhã (darei + o)
I shall give it tomorrow

When you use the indirect pronoun *lhe* or a combination of pronouns with *lh-* you do not need to remove the *r* from the future or conditional form:

Eu dar-lhe-ei o lápis (darei + lhe)
I shall give the pencil to him

Eu dar-lho-ia com muito gosto (daria + lho)
I would/should give it to him with great pleasure

But:

Eu dá-lo-ia com muito gosto (daria + o)
I would/should give it with great pleasure

Reflexive pronouns

Singular

me myself
te yourself (familiar)
se yourself (formal/informal),
   himself, herself, itself

Plural

nos ourselves
vos yourselves (obsolete)
se yourselves (formal/
   informal), themselves

Did you notice that the first and second person pronouns are exactly the same as the direct and indirect object pronouns (see previous section)?

The reflexive pronouns are used with the reflexive verbs, as described above in the section 'What is a verb? General structure'. In an affirmative sentence where the subject is not preceded by adverbs, prepositions, etc., the reflexive pronoun comes after the verb, linked to it by a hyphen (in the same way as an object pronoun):

sinto-me bem
I feel well

sentamo-nos
we sit

Note how the 'we' form of the verb loses its final *s* before the reflexive pronoun.

If the subject is preceded by an adverb, preposition or conjunction, the reflexive (or object) pronoun will come before the verb. The same applies when the sentence is in the negative or subjunctive.

Antes de me ir embora...
Before I go away...

Ela sempre se lavou com água fria
She has always washed (herself) in cold water

Nunca me esquecerei de ti
I shall never forget you

Se me divertisse... (subjunctive)
If I enjoyed/should enjoy myself...

In compound tenses the reflexive pronoun follows the auxiliary verb, never the past participle:

Eu tenho-me lembrado muitas vezes
I have remembered (it) many times

In the future and the conditional the pronoun, like the object pronouns, is inserted between the *r* of the verb and its ending:

Levantar-me-ei às nove horas
I shall get up at nine o'clock

Eles levantar-se-iam...
They would get up...

The reflexive pronouns are also used to express reciprocal actions (involving 'each other'), for example:

Eles amam-se
They love each other

Conhecemo-nos
We know each other

If it is not clear whether the action is reciprocal or reflexive, one can add other words for emphasis. If in the first example above the meaning was 'They love themselves' instead of 'each other', one might say *Eles amam-se a si próprios*. Similarly, the sentence *Conhecemo-nos* might also mean 'we know ourselves', so to make the meaning clear we could add *um ao outro* 'each other'. Note these different forms:

uma à outra (two females)	*umas às outras* (several females)
um ao outro (two males or mixed)	*uns aos outros* (several males or mixed)

Here are some more examples:

Eles enganam-se
They make a mistake

(*Enganar-se* is a reflexive verb meaning 'to make a mistake'.)

Eles enganam-se um ao outro
They deceive each other

(This time the verb is *enganar,* meaning 'to deceive', using *se* as a reciprocal pronoun.)

Se may also appear in a different capacity, as the impersonal subject. This is equivalent to the French 'on' and translates the English 'one', 'they' or the passive voice ('it is said', etc.) when it is not known *(quando não se sabe)* who the true subject is.

Aqui fala-se inglês
English is spoken here

Diz-se que ela é muito rica
It is said/They say that she is very rich

Vê-se muita gente nas lojas
One sees a lot of people in the shops

Accents and stress

Remember that Portuguese words are automatically stressed on the last but one syllable unless there is an accent mark elsewhere or unless the form ends in an *r, l, z, i* or a diphthong (such as *ou, ei*). For example:

fala, falar, falei, falou, falávamos, falaram, falarão

In these last two forms, belonging respectively to the past definite and the future, the sound of the final syllable is the same, but the words sound different because the stress falls in a different place. In the past definite *falaram* it falls on the last but one syllable, making the sound of the middle *a* open (like 'ah'); in the future *falarão* the stress falls on the last syllable, so that the unstressed middle *a* becomes mute (like 'e' in 'mother').

It is therefore important to write the accents whenever they are required. For example, do not forget to put accents on the second and third person singular future forms — *falará, falarás* - otherwise they will be read as the simple pluperfect: *falara, falaras*.

Look at the difference between *falamos* (we speak - present) and *falámos* (we spoke - past definite). In this case the two forms are both stressed on the second syllable, but are distinguished by the written accent, which makes the second *a* open. (Usually the *a* before *m* is mute even when the stress falls on it, unless of course it has an accent.)

All imperfect and conditional tenses have accents on the first (and second) person plural forms:

tínhamos, tínheis, teríamos, teríeis, falávamos, faláveis

This applies to the imperfect subjunctive as well as the indicative (see the section on 'Tenses'):

falássemos, partísseis, trouxéssemos, fôssemos

Interrogative form

We have mentioned that the English auxiliary 'do', used in forming questions, has no equivalent in Portuguese (see the section 'Auxiliaries: Translating English auxiliaries'). In Portuguese questions the word order is generally the same as in the affirmative; the only change is in the inflection of the voice:

Ele fala inglês   *Ele fala inglês?*
He speaks English   Does he speak English?

Sometimes, especially when the sentence begins with an interrogative word ('what? who?' etc.), the subject pronoun comes after the verb:

Ela vai...   *Quando vai ela?*
She is going...   When is she going?

Part II

Model conjugations of regular verbs

IMPERSONAL INFINITIVE:
falar *to speak*　　　**vender** *to sell*　　　**partir** to leave

PAST PARTICIPLE:
falado　　　vendido　　　partido

PRESENT PARTICIPLE (GERUND):
falando　　　vendendo　　　partindo

COMPOUND PRESENT PARTICIPLE (COMPOUND GERUND):
tendo falado　　　tendo vendido　　　tendo partido

Indicative mood

PRESENT:

eu *I* falo		vendo	parto
tu *you* falas		vendes	partes
você *you*			
o senhor *you*	fala	vende	parte
ele, ela *he, she*			
nós *we* falamos		vendemos	partimos
(vós *ye* falais)		(vendeis)	(partis)
vocês *you*			
os senhores *you*	falam	vendem	partem
eles, elas *they*			

No subject pronouns will be used from now on. Please see the table of pronouns in the section 'Subject pronouns'.

PAST DEFINITE:

falei	vendi	parti
falaste	vendeste	partiste
falou	vendeu	partiu
falámos	vendemos	partimos
(falastes)	(vendestes)	(partistes)
falaram	venderam	partiram

Note that the past definite of the 2nd and 3rd conjugations in the first person plural (we) is the same as the present tense. In the 1st conjugation it is distinguished by an accent in the past definite (see section on 'Accents and stress').

IMPERFECT:

falava	vendia	partia
falavas	vendias	partias
falava	vendia	partia
falávamos	vendíamos	partíamos
(faláveis)	(vendíeis)	(partíeis)
falavam	vendiam	partiam

Do not forget the acute accent on the first person plural as well as on the obsolete second person plural form.

PERFECT:

tenho			
tens			
tem	falado	vendido	partido
temos			
(tendes)			
têm			

41

SIMPLE PLUPERFECT *(not used in speech):*

falara	vendera	partira
falaras	venderas	partiras
falara	vendera	partira
faláramos	vendêramos	partíramos
(faláreis)	(vendêreis)	(partíreis)
falaram	venderam	partiram

Once again there are accents on the first and second persons plural. The last person, the third person plural, is the same as in the past definite.

COMPOUND PLUPERFECT:

tinha			
tinhas			
tinha			
tínhamos	falado	vendido	partido
(tínheis)			
tinham			

SIMPLE FUTURE:

falarei	venderei	partirei
falarás	venderás	partirás
falará	venderá	partirá
falaremos	venderemos	partiremos
(falareis)	(vendereis)	(partireis)
falarão	venderão	partirão

Compare the future with the simple pluperfect and note the different position of the stress. In the third person plural the stress is on the last syllable, instead of the penultimate as is the case with the other tenses where this form ends in -am.

COMPOUND FUTURE (FUTURE PERFECT):

terei			
terás			
terá	falado	vendido	partido
teremos			
(tereis)			
terão			

SIMPLE CONDITIONAL:

falaria	venderia	partiria
falarias	venderias	partirias
falaria	venderia	partiria
falaríamos	venderíamos	partiríamos
(falaríeis)	(venderíeis)	(partiríeis)
falariam	venderiam	partiriam

COMPOUND CONDITIONAL (CONDITIONAL PERFECT):

teria			
terias			
teria	falado	vendido	partido
teríamos			
(teríeis)			
teriam			

Subjunctive mood

PRESENT:

fale	venda	parta
fales	vendas	partas
fale	venda	parta
falemos	vendamos	partamos
(faleis)	(vendais)	(partais)
falem	vendam	partam

IMPERFECT:

falasse	vendesse	partisse
falasses	vendesses	partisses
falasse	vendesse	partisse
falássemos	vendêssemos	partíssemos
(falásseis)	(vendêsseis)	(partísseis)
falassem	vendessem	partissem

Note the accents once again in the first (and second) persons plural, and the fact that in the 2nd conjugation the accent is a circumflex: -ê-.

(COMPOUND) PERFECT:

tenha
tenhas
tenha
tenhamos } falado   vendido   partido
tenhais
tenham

(COMPOUND) PLUPERFECT:

tivesse
tivesses
tivesse
tivéssemos } falado   vendido   partido
(tivésseis)
tivessem

44

SIMPLE FUTURE:

falar	vender	partir
falares	venderes	partires
falar	vender	partir
falarmos	vendermos	partirmos
(falardes)	(venderdes)	(partirdes)
falarem	venderem	partirem

The personal infinitive is conjugated exactly as the simple future.

COMPOUND FUTURE (FUTURE PERFECT):

tiver			
tiveres			
tiver	falado	vendido	partido
tivermos			
(tiverdes)			
tiverem			

Imperative mood

The imperative proper has only two persons:

fala (tu)	vende (tu)	parte (tu)
falai (vós)	vendei (vós)	parti (vós)

All other persons in the imperative (i.e. 'we' and the polite forms) use the present subjunctive:

fale (você,	venda (você,	parta (você,
o senhor)	o senhor)	o senhor)
falemos (nós)	vendamos (nós)	partamos (nós)
falem (vocês,	vendam (vocês,	partam (vocês,
os senhores)	os senhores)	os senhores)

In negative commands, all persons use the present subjunctive.

Model conjugation of a reflexive verb

IMPERSONAL INFINITIVE:
sentar-se *to sit down*

PAST PARTICIPLE:
sentado *sat down*

PRESENT PARTICIPLE (GERUND):
sentando-se *sitting down*

COMPOUND PRESENT PARTICIPLE (COMPOUND GERUND):
tendo-se sentado *having sat down*

Indicative mood

PRESENT:

eu	sento-me	*I sit (myself) down,*
tu	sentas-te	*etc.*
você, ele	senta-se	
nós	sentamo-nos	
(vós	sentais-vos)	
vocês, eles	sentam-se	

A standard translation is given for guidance only. For full details of the use of each tense, see the section on 'Tenses' in Part I.

PAST DEFINITE:

eu	sentei-me	*I sat (myself) down,*
tu	sentaste-te	*or I have sat*
você, ele	sentou-se	*(myself) down, etc.*
nós	sentámo-nos	
(vós	sentastes-vos)	
vocês, eles	sentaram-se	

IMPERFECT:

eu	sentava-me	*I was sitting (myself)*
tu	sentavas-te	*down, etc.*
você, ele	sentava-se	
nós	sentávamo-nos	
(vós	sentáveis-vos)	
vocês, eles	sentavam-se	

PERFECT:

eu	tenho-me		*I have been sitting*
tu	tens-te		*(myself) down, etc.*
você, ele	tem-se		
nós	temo-nos	sentado	
(vós	tendes-vos)		
vocês, eles	têm-se		

SIMPLE PLUPERFECT *(not used in speech):*

eu	sentara-me	*I had sat (myself)*
tu	sentaras-te	*down, etc.*
você, ele	sentara-se	
nós	sentáramo-nos	
(vós	sentáreis-vos)	
vocês, eles	sentaram-se	

COMPOUND PLUPERFECT:

eu	tinha-me	*I had sat (myself)*
tu	tinhas-te	*down, etc.*
você, ele	tinha-se	
nós	tínhamo-nos sentado	
(vós	tínheis-vos)	
vocês, eles	tinham-se	

SIMPLE FUTURE:

eu	sentar-me-ei	*I shall sit (myself)*
tu	sentar-te-ás	*down, etc.*
você, ele	sentar-se-á	
nós	sentar-nos-emos	
(vós	sentar-vos-eis)	
vocês, eles	sentar-se-ão	

For the position of the reflexive pronouns in this and the following tenses, see the section 'Object pronouns and pronominal tenses' in Part I.

COMPOUND FUTURE (FUTURE PERFECT):

eu	ter-me-ei	*I shall have sat*
tu	ter-te-ás	*(myself) down, etc.*
você, ele	ter-se-á	
nós	ter-nos-emos sentado	
(vós	ter-vos-eis)	
vocês, eles	ter-se-ão	

SIMPLE CONDITIONAL:

eu	sentar-me-ia	*I should sit (myself)*
tu	sentar-te-ias	*down, etc.*
você, ele	sentar-se-ia	
nós	sentar-nos-íamos	
(vós	sentar-vos-íeis)	
vocês, eles	sentar-se-iam	

COMPOUND CONDITIONAL (CONDITIONAL PERFECT):

eu	ter-me-ia	*I should have sat*
tu	ter-te-ias	*(myself) down, etc.*
você, ele	ter-se-ia	
nós	ter-nos-íamos sentado	
(vós	ter-vos-íeis)	
vocês, eles	ter-se-iam	

Subjunctive mood

PRESENT:

eu	me	sente	*I may sit (myself)*
tu	te	sentes	*down, etc.*
você, ele	se	sente	
nós	nos	sentemos	
(vós	vos	senteis)	
vocês, eles	se	sentem	

IMPERFECT:

eu	me	sentasse	*I might sit (myself)*
tu	te	sentasses	*down, etc.*
você, ele	se	sentasse	
nós	nos	sentássemos	
(vós	vos	sentásseis)	
vocês, eles	se	sentassem	

(COMPOUND) PERFECT:

eu	me	tenha	*I may have sat*
tu	te	tenhas	*(myself) down, etc.*
você, ele	se	tenha	
nós	nos	tenhamos sentado	
(vós	vos	tenhais)	
vocês, eles	se	tenham	

(COMPOUND) PLUPERFECT:

eu	me	tivesse	*I might have sat*
tu	te	tivesses	*(myself) down, etc.*
você, ele	se	tivesse	
nós	nos	tivéssemos sentado	
(vós	vos	tivésseis)	
vocês, eles	se	tivessem	

SIMPLE FUTURE:

eu	me	sentar	*(if) I shall sit*
tu	te	sentares	*(myself) down, etc.*
você, ele	se	sentar	
nós	nos	sentarmos	
(vós	vos	sentardes)	
vocês, eles	se	sentarem	

The personal infinitive is conjugated exactly as the simple future.

COMPOUND FUTURE (FUTURE PERFECT):

eu	me	tiver	*(if) I shall have sat*
tu	te	tiveres	*(myself) down, etc.*
você, ele	se	tiver	
nós	nos	tivermos sentado	
(vós	vos	tiverdes)	
vocês, eles	se	tiverem	

COMPOUND PERSONAL INFINITIVE:

eu	me	ter	*(No equivalent in*
tu	te	teres	*English.)*
você, ele	se	ter	
nós	nos	termos sentado	
(vós	vos	terdes)	
vocês, eles	se	terem	

Imperative mood

| (tu) | senta-te | *sit down* |
| (vós) | sentai-vos | *sit down* |

All other persons in the imperative (i.e. 'we' and the polite forms) use the present subjunctive. In negative commands, all persons use the present subjunctive, and the reflexive pronoun comes before the verb instead of after as in the affirmative.

List of common reflexive verbs

aborrecer-se (de)	*to get bored (with)*
acostumar-se a	*to get used to*
afligir-se	*to get worried*
agitar-se	*to get excited, nervous, angry*
apressar-se	*to hurry*
aproximar-se (de)	*to approach*
arranjar-se	*to get ready, groom oneself*
arrepender-se (de)	*to repent, regret*
banhar-se	*to bathe*
barbear-se	*to shave oneself*
cansar-se (de)	*to get tired, tire (of)*
casar-se (com)	*to get married (to)*
chamar-se	*to be called*
decidir-se (a)	*to decide (to)*
deitar-se	*to lie down, go to bed*
despedir-se	*to take one's leave, say goodbye*
despir-se	*to get undressed*
divertir-se	*to enjoy oneself*
embriagar-se	*to get drunk*
encontrar-se (com)	*to meet (someone)*
enganar-se	*to make a mistake*
engasgar-se	*to choke*
entregar-se (a)	*to surrender oneself (to)*
entusiasmar-se	*to get excited, enthusiastic*
esquecer-se (de)	*to forget*
fingir-se	*to pretend to be*
habituar-se (a)	*to get used (to)*
importar-se	*to mind, be concerned*
ir-se embora	*to go away*
lamentar-se	*to lament*
lavar-se	*to wash oneself, have a wash*
lembrar-se (de)	*to remember*

levantar-se	*to get up*
mexer-se	*to move*
mover-se	*to move*
parecer-se (com)	*to look like*
pentear-se	*to comb one's hair*
preocupar-se	*to worry, be preoccupied*
queixar-se (de)	*to complain (about)*
recusar-se (a)	*to refuse (to)*
remediar-se	*to make do*
rir-se de	*to make fun of, laugh at*
sentar-se	*to sit down*
sentir-se	*to feel (well, ill, happy, etc.)*
servir-se (de)	*to help oneself (to), make use (of)*
submeter-se	*to submit oneself*
sujeitar-se	*to subject oneself*
sumir-se	*to vanish*
tratar-se de	*to be about, concern (something)*
vestir-se	*to get dressed*
zangar-se	*to be angry*

Part III

Defective, impersonal and unipersonal verbs

Defective verbs are those which lack some persons or tenses. As there are very few of them and most of those are seldom used, we shall only deal with one or two more common ones. The impersonal verbs are only used in the third person singular and the unipersonal verbs only in the third person singular and plural.

Jazer ('to lie at rest') outside poetry etc. is used mainly in the third person singular and plural of the present and imperfect tenses, both indicative and subjunctive. It is a regular verb. Examples:

Aqui jaz...   *Aqui jazem...*
Here lies...   Here lie...

O soldado jazia no campo de batalha
The soldier was lying on the battlefield

Prazer ('to please') is used mainly in the third person singular and in reference to God: *praz a Deus* - it pleases God. It is an irregular verb. Forms:

PRESENT INDICATIVE: *praz*   IMPERFECT INDICATIVE: *prazia*
PAST DEFINITE   PLUPERFECT INDICATIVE:
 INDICATIVE: *prouve*   *prouvera*
FUTURE INDICATIVE: *prazerá* CONDITIONAL: *prazeria*
FUTURE SUBJUNCTIVE: *prouver* PAST PARTICIPLE: *prazido*
PRESENT PARTICIPLE: *prazendo*

Reaver ('to have again') has no subjunctive. It is otherwise conjugated like *haver* (see the section 'Irregular verbs' below), except for the following forms:

PRESENT INDICATIVE: *nós reavemos, (vós reaveis)*
IMPERATIVE: No singular, plural *reavei vós*

Haver has three identities. As an auxiliary it has the same function and translation ('have') as *ter*, but is less commonly used; with *de*, conjugated in the present tense and followed by an infinitive, it implies an emphatic future, while in the imperfect tense, it expresses obligation. For these uses see the section 'Auxiliaries' in Part I. In its third use *haver* is an impersonal verb (only used in the third person singular of each tense) and corresponds to the English 'there is' or 'there are', or to the French 'il y a'. Forms:

PRESENT INDICATIVE: *há*	IMPERFECT INDICATIVE: *havia*
PAST DEFINITE INDICATIVE: *houve*	PLUPERFECT INDICATIVE: *houvera*
FUTURE INDICATIVE: *haverá*	CONDITIONAL: *haveria*
PRESENT SUBJUNCTIVE: *haja*	IMPERFECT SUBJUNCTIVE: *houvesse*
FUTURE SUBJUNCTIVE: *houver*	IMPERATIVE: *haja*
PAST PARTICIPLE: *havido*	PRESENT PARTICIPLE: *havendo*

Tratar-se de ('to be about') corresponds to the French 'il s'agit de', and is an impersonal verb naturally used only in the third person singular. Examples:

De que se trata isso?
What is it about?

De que se tratava o filme? Tratava-se duma guerra.
What was the film about? It was about war.

There are other impersonal verbs referring to the weather: *nevar* 'to snow' (regular), *chover* 'to rain' (regular) and so on. Similarly, the irregular verb *fazer* is impersonal in phrases like the following:

faz sol	*faz calor*	*faz frio*	*faz vento*
it is sunny	it is hot	it is cold	it is windy

Unipersonal verbs (used only in the third person singular and plural) mostly relate to the sounds made by animals:

o gato mia	*os lobos uivam*	*dói*
the cat mews	the wolves howl	it hurts

Radical-changing and orthographical-changing verbs

Radical-changing verbs

Truly irregular verbs are few, but there are numerous verbs, mostly ending in -*ir*, which have slight irregularities in the present indicative tense in certain persons (usually only the first person singular) and consequently also in all persons of the present subjunctive. They divide for easier learning into five groups (plus a few which fall outside these).

e to i

In the following 3rd conjugation verbs (-*ir* verbs), where the vowel preceding the ending has an *e*, you change this *e* to an *i* in the first person only of the present indicative:

INFINITIVE:	INDICATIVE:	SUBJUNCTIVE:
seguir *to follow, go on*	sigo	siga
	segues	sigas
	segue	siga
	seguimos	sigamos
	(seguis)	(sigais)
	seguem	sigam

The following verbs are also conjugated in the same way: consult the tables of regular verbs in Part II for the full subjunctive forms.

despir *to undress*	dispo	dispa *etc.*
despir-se *to get undressed*	dispo-me	me dispa *etc.*
divertir *to amuse*	divirto	divirta *etc.*
divertir-se *to enjoy*	divirto-me	me divirta *etc.*
ferir *to wound, hurt*	firo	fira *etc.*
mentir *to lie*	minto	minta *etc.*
preferir *to prefer*	prefiro	prefira *etc.*
reflectir *to reflect*	reflicto	reflicta *etc.*
repetir *to repeat*	repito	repita *etc.*

sentir *to feel*	sinto	sinta *etc.*
sentir-se *to feel (well,* etc.*)*	sinto-me	me sinta *etc.*
servir *to serve*	sirvo	sirva *etc.*
servir-se *to help oneself*	sirvo-me	me sirva *etc.*
transferir *to transfer*	transfiro	transfira *etc.*
vestir *to dress*	visto	vista *etc.*
vestir-se *to get dressed*	visto-me	me vista *etc.*

The verbs *conseguir* ('to achieve') and *perseguir* ('to chase, harass') are conjugated like *seguir. These verbs have the further peculiarity of losing the* u *following the* g; *this is explained in the following section on 'Orthographical-changing verbs'.*

Agredir ('to assault'), *prevenir* ('to warn'), *progredir* ('to progress') and *transgredir* ('to transgress') keep the *i* change in all three persons singular and third plural of the present indicative, as well as throughout the subjunctive.

INFINITIVE:	INDICATIVE:	SUBJUNCTIVE:
agredir *to assault*	agrido	agrida
	agrides	agridas
	agride	agrida
	agredimos	agridamos
	(agredis)	(agridais)
	agridem	agridam

u to o
The following verbs change the *u* to an *o* in the second and third person singular and the third person plural of the present indicative:

INFINITIVE:	INDICATIVE:	SUBJUNCTIVE:
subir *to go up*	subo	suba
	sobes	subas
	sobe	suba
	subimos	subamos
	(subis)	(subais)
	sobem	subam

In the same way: *acudir* 'to aid', *construir* 'to build', *consumir* 'to consume'.

cuspir *to spit*	cuspo, cospes	cuspa
destruir *to destroy*	destruo, destróis	destrua
fugir *to flee*	fujo, foges	fuja
sacudir *to shake off*	sacudo, sacodes	sacuda
sumir-se *to vanish*	sumo-me, somes-te	me suma

Note the spelling change in fujo, fuja *etc.: see the following section.*

• Other verbs ending in *-ir* but preceded by *u* are conjugated as *diminuir* ('to lessen'): *diminuo, diminuis, diminui, diminuimos, (diminuis,) diminuem.* Subjunctive: *diminua etc*

• Verbs ending in *-ir* but preceded by *a* are conjugated as *cair* ('to fall'): *caio, cais, cai, caimos, (caís), caem.* Subjunctive: *caia etc.*

o to u
The following verbs change the *o* to a *u* in the first person singular of the present indicative:

INFINITIVE:	INDICATIVE:	SUBJUNCTIVE:
dormir *to sleep*	durmo	durma
	dormes	durmas
	dorme	durma
	dormimos	durmamos
	(dormis)	(durmais)
	dormem	durmam

In the same way: cobrir *to cover,* descobrir *to discover,* engolir *to swallow,* tossir *to cough.*

iar to ei

INFINITIVE:	INDICATIVE:	SUBJUNCTIVE:
odiar *to hate*	odeio	odeie
	odeias	odeies
	odeia	odeie
	odiamos	odiemos
	(odiais)	(odieis)
	odeiam	odeiem

In the same way: ansiar *to yearn for,* incendiar *to set fire to,* remediar *to rectify. Other verbs in -iar are regular.*

The verbs crer ('to believe') *and* ler ('to read') *follow a similar but slightly different pattern. Crer is given as an example:*

INFINITIVE:	INDICATIVE:	SUBJUNCTIVE:
crer *to believe*	creio	creia
	crês	creias
	crê	creia
	cremos	creiamos
	(credes)	(creiais)
	crêem	creiam

ear to ei

INFINITIVE:	INDICATIVE:	SUBJUNCTIVE:
passear *to go for a walk*	passeio	passeie
	passeias	passeies
	passeia	passeie
	passeamos	passeemos
	(passeais)	(passeeis)
	passeiam	passeiem

All verbs in -ear follow this pattern, e.g. barbear *to shave,* cear *to have supper,* estrear *to do first,* pentear *to comb,* pentear-se *to comb one's hair,* recear *to fear.*

Other verbs
These verbs have irregular forms only in the first person singular of the present indicative, and consequently also in the subjunctive:

INFINITIVE:	INDICATIVE:	SUBJUNCTIVE:
medir *to measure*	meço	meça
ouvir *to hear*	ouço/oiço	ouça/oiça
pedir *to ask for*	peço	peça
perder *to lose*	perco	perca
valer *to be worth*	valho	valha

59

The verb *remir* ('to redeem') is in a class of its own:

INFINITIVE:	INDICATIVE:	SUBJUNCTIVE:
remir *to redeem*	redimo	redima
	redimes	redimas
	redime	redima
	remimos	redimamos
	(remis)	(redimais)
	redimem	redimam

In other tenses the stem of the infinitive is used, except in the imperative:
redime (tu), remi (vós).

Verbs in *-uzir* are considered regular, but to make it quite clear, here is
one example conjugated:

INFINITIVE:	INDICATIVE:	SUBJUNCTIVE:
conduzir *to drive,*	conduzo	conduza
conduct	conduzes	conduzas
	conduz	conduza
	conduzimos	conduzamos
	(conduzis)	(conduzais)
	conduzem	conduzam

Verbs in *-oar* are regular but note the circumflex accent in the first person: *voar* to fly, *vôo* I fly; *soar* to sound, *sôo* I sound.

Verbs in *-oer* (*moer* 'to grind', *roer* 'to gnaw', *doer* 'to hurt') follow this
pattern:

INFINITIVE:	INDICATIVE:	SUBJUNCTIVE:
roer *to gnaw*	rôo	roa
	rois	roas
	roi	roa
	roemos	roamos
	(roeis)	(roais)
	roem	roam

In all other tenses keep the o *before adding the respective regular endings.*
Doer *is a unipersonal verb (see the previous section).*

Orthographical-changing verbs

In these verbs the last consonant of the stem is modified or changed in certain persons and tenses in order to preserve the sound of the infinitive. The patterns are as follows:

INFINITIVE ENDING IN:	-car	-çar	-cer	-gar	-ger/ -gir	-guer/ -guir
CHANGES TO:						
BEFORE a, o	-	-	ç	-	j	g
BEFORE e, i	qu	c	-	gu	-	-

Examples:
ficar - fique, alcançar - alcancei, conhecer - conheço/conheça, alugar - aluguei, fugir - fujo/fuja, seguir - sigo/siga.

Irregular verbs

For ease of learning, groups of verbs which follow a similar pattern will be presented together first. This means that two verbs which are grouped together as having a similar present tense may not be together in the past definite groupings if their past definites are different. If any tense of a particular verb does not appear here, it means that it is regular. In the following section, all the irregular verbs will be listed alphabetically and conjugated fully in the traditional manner.

Groups of verbs

PRESENT INDICATIVE:

ser *to be*	sou	és	é	somos	(sois)	são
estar *to be*	estou	estás	está	estamos	(estais)	estão
dar *to give*	dou	dás	dá	damos	(dais)	dão
ir *to go*	vou	vais	vai	vamos	(ides)	vão

ter *to have*	tenho	tens	tem	temos	(tendes)	têm
vir *to come*	venho	vens	vem	vimos	(vindes)	vêm

haver *to have*	hei	hás	há	havemos	(haveis)	hão

The last person resembles the first group above, but the first three are like saber, which follows.

These have a regular present tense, apart from the first person. (Note the lack of an -e ending in the third person singular after a z.)

saber *to know*	sei	sabes	sabe	sabemos	(sabeis)	sabem
caber *to fit in*	caibo	cabes	cabe	cabemos	(cabeis)	cabem
trazer *to bring*	trago	trazes	traz	trazemos	(trazeis)	trazem
dizer *to say*	digo	dizes	diz	dizemos	(dizeis)	dizem
fazer *to do*	faço	fazes	faz	fazemos	(fazeis)	fazem
poder *to be able*	posso	podes	pode	podemos	(podeis)	podem

pôr *to put*	ponho	pões	põe	pomos	(pondes)	põem

rir *to laugh*	rio	ris	ri	rimos	(rides)	riem

ver *to see*	vejo	vês	vê	vemos	(vedes)	vêem

querer *to want*	quero	queres	quer	queremos	(quereis)	querem

This verb is regular in the present tense, but not in the past definite or the subjunctive. (Note the lack of an -e ending in quer.)

PAST DEFINITE INDICATIVE:

ter	tive	tiveste	teve	tivemos	(tivestes)	tiveram
estar	estive	estiveste	esteve	estivemos	(estivestes)	estiveram

querer	quis	quiseste	quis	quisemos	(quisestes)	quiseram
fazer	fiz	fizeste	fez	fizemos	(fizestes)	fizeram

saber	soube	soubeste	soube	soubemos	(soubestes)	souberam
caber	coube	coubeste	coube	coubemos	(coubestes)	couberam
haver	houve	houveste	houve	houvemos	(houvestes)	houveram
trazer	trouxe	trouxeste	trouxe	trouxemos	(trouxestes)	trouxeram

dizer	disse	disseste	disse	dissemos	(dissestes)	disseram

ver	vi	viste	viu	vimos	(vistes)	viram

Note that the first person plural past definite of ver *(vimos we saw) is the same as the first person plural present tense of* vir *(vimos we come).*

vir	vim	vieste	veio	viemos	(viestes)	vieram
poder	pude	pudeste	pôde	pudemos	(pudestes)	puderam
pôr	pus	puseste	pôs	pusemos	(pusestes)	puseram

ir ⎱						
	fui	foste	foi	fomos	(fostes)	foram
ser ⎰						

Note that the Portuguese for 'went' and for 'was/were' is the same.

dar	dei	deste	deu	demos	(destes)	deram

IMPERFECT:

Most irregular verbs form the remaining tenses in the regular way (see Part I, 'Tenses' for formation) so from this point on only those verbs which show irregularities in each tense are listed.

ser *to be*	era	eras	era	éramos	(éreis)	eram
pôr *to put*	punha	punhas	punha	púnhamos	(púnheis)	punham
ter *to have*	tinha	tinhas	tinha	tínhamos	(tínheis)	tinham
vir *to come*	vinha	vinhas	vinha	vínhamos	(vínheis)	vinham

FUTURE:

dizer *to tell*	direi	dirás	dirá	diremos	(direis)	dirão
fazer *to do*	farei	farás	fará	faremos	(fareis)	farão
trazer *to bring*	trarei	trarás	trará	traremos	(trareis)	trarão

These verbs form the conditional from these irregular future stems, adding the regular endings: diria, faria, traria etc. (See 'Tenses' in Part I.)

PRESENT SUBJUNCTIVE:

Irregular verbs form this tense from the first person of the present indicative, with the following exceptions:

dar *to give*	dê	dês	dê	demos	(deis)	dêem
estar *to be*	esteja	estejas	esteja	estejamos	(estejais)	estejam
haver *to have*	haja	hajas	haja	hajamos	(hajais)	hajam
ir *to go*	vá	vás	vá	vamos	(vades)	vão
querer *to want*	queira	queiras	queira	queiramos	(queirais)	queiram
saber *to know*	saiba	saibas	saiba	saibamos	(saibais)	saibam
ser *to be*	seja	sejas	seja	sejamos	(sejais)	sejam

IMPERFECT SUBJUNCTIVE:

Formed from the first person of the past definite indicative, except:

dar *to give*	desse	desses	desse	déssemos	(désseis)	dessem
ir *to go* } ser *to be* }	fosse	fosses	fosse	fôssemos	(fôsseis)	fossem
vir *to come*	viesse	viesses	viesse	viéssemos	(viésseis)	viessem

These verbs form the future subjunctive like the imperfect subjunctive, adding the regular endings: der, for, vier etc. (See 'Tenses' in Part I.)

PAST PARTICIPLE:

For a list of irregular past participles, see the section on 'Tenses: past participle and passive tenses' in Part I.

Alphabetical list of conjugated irregular verbs

caber	PRESENT	PAST DEFINITE:	IMPERFECT:
to fit in	INDIC:		
	caibo	coube	cabia
	cabes	coubeste	cabias
	cabe	coube	cabia
	cabemos	coubemos	cabíamos
	(cabeis)	(coubestes)	(cabíeis)
	cabem	couberam	cabiam

PARTICIPLES:	FUTURE:	CONDITIONAL:	IMPERATIVE:
cabendo	caberei	caberia	*none*
cabido	caberás	caberias	
	caberá	caberia	
	caberemos	caberíamos	
	(cabereis)	(caberíeis)	
	caberão	caberiam	

PERSONAL	PRESENT	IMPERFECT	FUTURE
INFINITIVE:	SUBJUNCTIVE:	SUBJUNCTIVE:	SUBJUNCTIVE:
caber	caiba	coubesse	couber
caberes	caibas	coubesses	couberes
caber	caiba	coubesse	couber
cabermos	caibamos	coubéssemos	coubermos
(caberdes)	(caibais)	(coubésseis)	(couberdes)
caberem	caibam	coubessem	couberem

dar	PRESENT	PAST DEFINITE:	IMPERFECT:
to give	INDIC:		
	dou	dei	dava
	dás	deste	davas
	dá	deu	dava
	damos	demos	dávamos
	(dais)	(destes)	(dáveis)
	dão	deram	davam

PARTICIPLES:	FUTURE:	CONDITIONAL:	IMPERATIVE:
dando	darei	daria	
dado	darás	darias	dá
	dará	daria	
	daremos	daríamos	
	(dareis)	(daríeis)	(dai)
	darão	dariam	

PERSONAL INFINITIVE:	PRESENT SUBJUNCTIVE:	IMPERFECT SUBJUNCTIVE:	FUTURE SUBJUNCTIVE:
dar	dê	desse	der
dares	dês	desses	deres
dar	dê	desse	der
darmos	demos	déssemos	dermos
(dardes)	(deis)	(désseis)	(derdes)
darem	dêem	dessem	derem

dizer	PRESENT	PAST DEFINITE:	IMPERFECT:
to tell	INDIC:		
	digo	disse	dizia
	dizes	disseste	dizias
	diz	disse	dizia
	dizemos	dissemos	dizíamos
	(dizeis)	(dissestes)	(dizíeis)
	dizem	disseram	diziam

PARTICIPLES:	FUTURE:	CONDITIONAL:	IMPERATIVE:
dizendo	direi	diria	
dito	dirás	dirias	diz(e)
	dirá	diria	
	diremos	diríamos	
	(direis)	(diríeis)	(dizei)
	dirão	diriam	

PERSONAL INFINITIVE:	PRESENT SUBJUNCTIVE:	IMPERFECT SUBJUNCTIVE:	FUTURE SUBJUNCTIVE:
dizer	diga	dissesse	disser
dizeres	digas	dissesses	disseres
dizer	diga	dissesse	disser
dizermos	digamos	disséssemos	dissermos
(dizerdes)	(digais)	(dissésseis)	(disserdes)
dizerem	digam	dissessem	disserem

estar	PRESENT	PAST DEFINITE:	IMPERFECT:
to be	INDIC:		
	estou	estive	estava
	estás	estiveste	estavas
	está	esteve	estava
	estamos	estivemos	estávamos
	(estais)	(estivestes)	(estáveis)
	estão	estiveram	estavam

PARTICIPLES:	FUTURE:	CONDITIONAL:	IMPERATIVE:
estando	estarei	estaria	
estado	estarás	estarias	está
	estará	estaria	
	estaremos	estaríamos	
	(estareis)	(estaríeis)	(estai)
	estarão	estariam	

PERSONAL	PRESENT	IMPERFECT	FUTURE
INFINITIVE:	SUBJUNCTIVE:	SUBJUNCTIVE:	SUBJUNCTIVE:
estar	esteja	estivesse	estiver
estares	estejas	estivesses	estiveres
estar	esteja	estivesse	estiver
estarmos	estejamos	estivéssemos	estivermos
(estardes)	(estejais)	(estivésseis)	(estiverdes)
estarem	estejam	estivessem	estiverem

fazer	PRESENT	PAST DEFINITE:	IMPERFECT:
to do	INDIC:		
	faço	fiz	fazia
	fazes	fizeste	fazias
	faz	fez	fazia
	fazemos	fizemos	fazíamos
	(fazeis)	(fizestes)	(fazíeis)
	fazem	fizeram	faziam

PARTICIPLES:	FUTURE:	CONDITIONAL:	IMPERATIVE:
fazendo	farei	faria	
feito	farás	farias	faz(e)
	fará	faria	
	faremos	fariamos	
	(fareis)	(faríeis)	(fazei)
	farão	fariam	

PERSONAL	PRESENT	IMPERFECT	FUTURE
INFINITIVE:	SUBJUNCTIVE:	SUBJUNCTIVE:	SUBJUNCTIVE:
fazer	faça	fizesse	fizer
fazeres	faças	fizesses	fizeres
fazer	faça	fizesse	fizer
fazermos	façamos	fizéssemos	fizermos
(fazerdes)	(façais)	(fizésseis)	(fizerdes)
fazerem	façam	fizessem	fizerem

haver	PRESENT	PAST DEFINITE:	IMPERFECT:
to have	INDIC:		
	hei	houve	havia
	hás	houveste	havias
	há	houve	havia
	havemos	houvemos	havíamos
	(haveis)	(houvestes)	(havíeis)
	hão	houveram	haviam

PARTICIPLES:	FUTURE:	CONDITIONAL:	IMPERATIVE:
havendo	haverei	haveria	
havido	haverás	haverias	há
	haverá	haveria	
	haveremos	haveríamos	
	(havereis)	(haveríeis)	(havei)
	haverão	haveriam	

PERSONAL	PRESENT	IMPERFECT	FUTURE
INFINITIVE:	SUBJUNCTIVE:	SUBJUNCTIVE:	SUBJUNCTIVE:
haver	haja	houvesse	houver
haveres	hajas	houvesses	houveres
haver	haja	houvesse	houver
havermos	hajamos	houvéssemos	houvermos
(haverdes)	(hajais)	(houvésseis)	(houverdes)
haverem	hajam	houvessem	houverem

ir	PRESENT	PAST DEFINITE:	IMPERFECT:
to go	INDIC:		
	vou	fui	ia
	vais	foste	ias
	vai	foi	ia
	vamos	fomos	íamos
	(ides)	(fostes)	(íeis)
	vão	foram	iam

PARTICIPLES:	FUTURE:	CONDITIONAL:	IMPERATIVE:
indo	irei	iria	
ido	irás	irias	vai
	irá	iria	
	iremos	iríamos	
	(ireis)	(iríeis)	(ide)
	irão	iriam	

PERSONAL	PRESENT	IMPERFECT	FUTURE
INFINITIVE:	SUBJUNCTIVE:	SUBJUNCTIVE:	SUBJUNCTIVE:
ir	vá	fosse	for
ires	vás	fosses	fores
ir	vá	fosse	for
irmos	vamos	fôssemos	formos
(irdes)	(vades)	(fôsseis)	(fordes)
irem	vão	fossem	forem

poder
to be able

PRESENT INDIC:	PAST DEFINITE:	IMPERFECT:
posso	pude	podia
podes	pudeste	podias
pode	pôde	podia
podemos	pudemos	podíamos
(podeis)	(pudestes)	(podíeis)
podem	puderam	podiam

PARTICIPLES:	FUTURE:	CONDITIONAL:	IMPERATIVE:
podendo	poderei	poderia	
podido	poderás	poderias	pode
	poderá	poderia	
	poderemos	poderíamos	
	(podereis)	(poderíeis)	(podei)
	poderão	poderiam	

PERSONAL INFINITIVE:	PRESENT SUBJUNCTIVE:	IMPERFECT SUBJUNCTIVE:	FUTURE SUBJUNCTIVE:
poder	possa	pudesse	puder
poderes	possas	pudesses	puderes
poder	possa	pudesse	puder
podermos	possamos	pudéssemos	pudermos
(poderdes)	(possais)	(pudésseis)	(puderdes)
poderem	possam	pudessem	puderem

pôr	PRESENT	PAST DEFINITE:	IMPERFECT:
to put	INDIC:		
	ponho	pus	punha
	pões	puseste	punhas
	põe	pôs	punha
	pomos	pusemos	púnhamos
	(pondes)	(pusestes)	(púnheis)
	põem	puseram	punham

PARTICIPLES:	FUTURE:	CONDITIONAL:	IMPERATIVE:
pondo	porei	poria	
posto	porás	porias	põe
	porá	poria	
	poremos	poríamos	
	(poreis)	(poríeis)	(ponde)
	porão	poriam	

PERSONAL INFINITIVE:	PRESENT SUBJUNCTIVE:	IMPERFECT SUBJUNCTIVE:	FUTURE SUBJUNCTIVE:
pôr	ponha	pusesse	puser
pores	ponhas	pusesses	puseres
pôr	ponha	pusesse	puser
pormos	ponhamos	puséssemos	pusermos
(pordes)	(ponhais)	(pusésseis)	(puserdes)
porem	ponham	pusessem	puserem

querer	PRESENT	PAST DEFINITE:	IMPERFECT:
to want	INDIC:		
	quero	quis	queria
	queres	quiseste	querias
	quer	quis	queria
	queremos	quisemos	queríamos
	(quereis)	(quisestes)	(queríeis)
	querem	quiseram	queriam

PARTICIPLES:	FUTURE:	CONDITIONAL:	IMPERATIVE:
querendo	quererei	quereria	
querido	quererás	quererias	quer
	quererá	quereria	
	quereremos	quereríamos	
	(querereis)	(quereríeis)	(querei)
	quererão	quereriam	

PERSONAL INFINITIVE:	PRESENT SUBJUNCTIVE:	IMPERFECT SUBJUNCTIVE:	FUTURE SUBJUNCTIVE:
querer	queira	quisesse	quiser
quereres	queiras	quisesses	quiseres
querer	queira	quisesse	quiser
querermos	queiramos	quiséssemos	quisermos
(quererdes)	(queirais)	(quisésseis)	(quiserdes)
quererem	queiram	quisessem	quiserem

rir	PRESENT	PAST DEFINITE:	IMPERFECT:
to laugh	INDIC:		
	rio	ri	ria
	ris	riste	rias
	ri	riu	ria
	rimos	rimos	ríamos
	(rides)	(ristes)	(ríeis)
	riem	riram	riam

PARTICIPLES:	FUTURE:	CONDITIONAL:	IMPERATIVE:
rindo	rirei	riria	
rido	rirás	ririas	ri
	rirá	riria	
	riremos	riríamos	
	(rireis)	(riríeis)	(ride)
	rirão	ririam	

PERSONAL INFINITIVE:	PRESENT SUBJUNCTIVE:	IMPERFECT SUBJUNCTIVE:	FUTURE SUBJUNCTIVE:
rir	ria	risse	rir
rires	rias	risses	rires
rir	ria	risse	rir
rirmos	riamos	ríssemos	rirmos
(rirdes)	(riais)	(rísseis)	(rirdes)
rirem	riam	rissem	rirem

saber	PRESENT	PAST DEFINITE:	IMPERFECT:
to know	INDIC:		
	sei	soube	sabia
	sabes	soubeste	sabias
	sabe	soube	sabia
	sabemos	soubemos	sabíamos
	(sabeis)	(soubestes)	(sabíeis)
	sabem	souberam	sabiam

PARTICIPLES:	FUTURE:	CONDITIONAL:	IMPERATIVE:
sabendo	saberei	saberia	
sabido	saberás	saberias	sabe
	saberá	saberia	
	saberemos	saberíamos	
	(sabereis)	(saberíeis)	(sabei)
	saberão	saberiam	

PERSONAL INFINITIVE:	PRESENT SUBJUNCTIVE:	IMPERFECT SUBJUNCTIVE:	FUTURE SUBJUNCTIVE:
saber	saiba	soubesse	souber
saberes	saibas	soubesses	souberes
saber	saiba	soubesse	souber
sabermos	saibamos	soubéssemos	soubermos
(saberdes)	(saibais)	(soubésseis)	(souberdes)
saberem	saibam	soubessem	souberem

ser	PRESENT	PAST DEFINITE:	IMPERFECT:
to be	INDIC:		
	sou	fui	era
	és	foste	eras
	é	foi	era
	somos	fomos	éramos
	(sois)	(fostes)	(éreis)
	são	foram	eram

PARTICIPLES:	FUTURE:	CONDITIONAL:	IMPERATIVE:
sendo	serei	seria	
sido	serás	serias	sê
	será	seria	
	seremos	seríamos	
	(sereis)	(seríeis)	(sede)
	serão	seriam	

PERSONAL	PRESENT	IMPERFECT	FUTURE
INFINITIVE:	SUBJUNCTIVE:	SUBJUNCTIVE:	SUBJUNCTIVE:
ser	seja	fosse	for
seres	sejas	fosses	fores
ser	seja	fosse	for
sermos	sejamos	fôssemos	formos
(serdes)	(sejais)	(fôsseis)	(fordes)
serem	sejam	fossem	forem

ter	PRESENT	PAST DEFINITE:	IMPERFECT:
to have	INDIC:		
	tenho	tive	tinha
	tens	tiveste	tinhas
	tem	teve	tinha
	temos	tivemos	tínhamos
	(tendes)	(tivestes)	(tínheis)
	têm	tiveram	tinham

PARTICIPLES:	FUTURE:	CONDITIONAL:	IMPERATIVE:
tendo	terei	teria	
tido	terás	terias	tem
	terá	teria	
	teremos	teríamos	
	(tereis)	(teríeis)	(tende)
	terão	teriam	

PERSONAL INFINITIVE:	PRESENT SUBJUNCTIVE:	IMPERFECT SUBJUNCTIVE:	FUTURE SUBJUNCTIVE:
ter	tenha	tivesse	tiver
teres	tenhas	tivesses	tiveres
ter	tenha	tivesse	tiver
termos	tenhamos	tivéssemos	tivermos
(terdes)	(tenhais)	(tivésseis)	(tiverdes)
terem	tenham	tivessem	tiverem

trazer	PRESENT	PAST DEFINITE:	IMPERFECT:
to bring	INDIC:		
	trago	trouxe	trazia
	trazes	trouxeste	trazias
	traz	trouxe	trazia
	trazemos	trouxemos	trazíamos
	(trazeis)	(trouxestes)	(trazíeis)
	trazem	trouxeram	traziam

PARTICIPLES:	FUTURE:	CONDITIONAL:	IMPERATIVE:
trazendo	trarei	traria	
trazido	trarás	trarias	traz(e)
	trará	traria	
	traremos	traríamos	
	(trareis)	(traríeis)	(trazei)
	trarão	trariam	

PERSONAL INFINITIVE:	PRESENT SUBJUNCTIVE:	IMPERFECT SUBJUNCTIVE:	FUTURE SUBJUNCTIVE:
trazer	traga	trouxesse	trouxer
trazeres	tragas	trouxesses	trouxeres
trazer	traga	trouxesses	trouxer
trazermos	tragamos	trouxéssemos	trouxermos
(trazerdes)	(tragais)	(trouxésseis)	(trouxerdes)
trazerem	tragam	trouxessem	trouxerem

ver	PRESENT	PAST DEFINITE:	IMPERFECT:
to see	INDIC:		
	vejo	vi	via
	vês	viste	vias
	vê	viu	via
	vemos	vimos	víamos
	(vedes)	(vistes)	(víeis)
	vêem	viram	viam

PARTICIPLES:	FUTURE:	CONDITIONAL:	IMPERATIVE:
vendo	verei	veria	
visto	verás	verias	vê
	verá	veria	
	veremos	veríamos	
	(vereis)	(veríeis)	(vede)
	verão	veriam	

PERSONAL INFINITIVE:	PRESENT SUBJUNCTIVE:	IMPERFECT SUBJUNCTIVE:	FUTURE SUBJUNCTIVE:
ver	veja	visse	vir
veres	vejas	visses	vires
ver	veja	visse	vir
vermos	vejamos	víssemos	virmos
(verdes)	(vejais)	(vísseis)	(virdes)
verem	vejam	vissem	virem

vir	PRESENT	PAST DEFINITE:	IMPERFECT:
to come	INDIC:		
	venho	vim	vinha
	vens	vieste	vinhas
	vem	veio	vinha
	vimos	viemos	vínhamos
	(vindes)	(viestes)	(vínheis)
	vêm	vieram	vinham

PARTICIPLES:	FUTURE:	CONDITIONAL:	IMPERATIVE:
vindo	virei	viria	
vindo	virás	virias	vem
	virá	viria	
	viremos	viríamos	
	(vireis)	(viríeis)	(vinde)
	virão	viriam	

PERSONAL	PRESENT	IMPERFECT	FUTURE
INFINITIVE:	SUBJUNCTIVE:	SUBJUNCTIVE:	SUBJUNCTIVE.
vir	venha	viesse	vier
vires	venhas	viesses	vieres
vir	venha	viesse	vier
virmos	venhamos	viéssemos	viermos
(virdes)	(venhais)	(viésseis)	(vierdes)
virem	venham	viessem	vierem

Verbal idioms

dar

dar horas *to strike the hour*
dar corda ao relógio *to wind (up) the clock/watch*
dar baixa ao hospital *to be admitted into hospital (for treatment)*
O médico deu-lhe alta. *The doctor discharged him (from the hospital).*
A janela dá para o mar. *The window looks out on the sea.*
dar para *to have a flair for (anything)*
Ela dá para a música. *She has a flair for music.*
O polícia não deu por isso. *The police didn't notice it/weren't aware of it/didn't realize it.*
dar com *to come across, to bump into (someone)*
dar-se bem/mal em ... *to be well and happy/unhappy in ...(a place)*
dar-se bem/mal com ... *to get along well/badly with ...(someone)*
dar à luz *to give birth*
dar por certo *to take for granted*
Quem me dera! *How I wish! Would that I might!*
ao Deus dará *aimlessly (left to one's own fate)*
dar uma vista de olhos *to take a quick look at/glance through*
dar uma volta *to go for a walk*

deixar

Ele deixou de fumar. *He stopped smoking.*
Deixe-me em paz. *Leave me alone.*
Ela deixou as cartas para outro dia. *She put off (writing) the letters until another day.*
Elas deixaram as camas por fazer. *They left the beds unmade.*

estar

estar para sair *to be on the point of going out*
O teatro estava às moscas. *The theatre was left to the flies (i.e. without customers).*
O cinema estava à cunha. *The cinema was packed.*
O trabalho está por fazer. *The work remains undone.*
A gasolina está pela hora da morte. *Petrol has become very expensive.*
estar de boa maré/má maré *to be in a good mood/bad mood*
estar em dia com…*to be up to date with…(correspondence etc)*
estar com fome/sêde *to be hungry/thirsty*
estar com sono/frio/calor *to be sleepy/hot/cold*
estar com sorte/ciúmes/medo *to be lucky/jealous/afraid*
estar com pressa/vontade de/razão *to be in a hurry/to feel like/to be right*

fazer

fazer a barba *to shave oneself*
fazer anos *to have a birthday*
Ele faz trinta anos hoje. *He is thirty today.*
Faz bom/mau tempo. *The weather is good/bad.*
Ela só faz asneiras. *She only makes mistakes.*
Você fez muito bem/mal. *You did the right/wrong thing.*
Nadar faz bem à saúde. *Swimming is good for the health.*
fazer as vontades de … *to do the will of/to give in to the wishes of someone*
Farei o possível. *I will do my best.*
Que é feito dela? *What has happened to her/become of her?*
fazer-se de bobo *to play dumb*
fazer uma viagem *to take a trip/to go on a journey*

ficar

Este chapéu fica-lhe bem. *This hat suits you.*
Ele ficou bem no exame. *He passed the exam.*
Fica para a semana. *Let us make it next week.*
Fica para a outra vez. *We'll make it another time.*
Fique descansada. *Don't worry, rest assured.*
Fico contente. *I am so happy (in respect of some news just learnt).*
Isto fica entre nós. *This is between us.*
Ele ficou sem dinheiro. *He was left without money.*

ir

ir ter com *to go to meet*
ir de encontro a *to collide with*
ir de avião/de autocarro *(in Brazil:* omnibus)/de barco *to fly/to go by bus/boat*
ir a pé/a cavalo *to walk, to go on foot/ride*
Vai mal de saúde. *He is in poor health. (Also:* Está muito mal.)
Como vão? *How are you (pl.)?*
Ir a Roma e não ver o Papa. *To go to Rome and not see the Pope (i.e. not to accomplish one's mission or purpose.)*
Ela vai aos ares. *She hits the ceiling/blows up in a rage.*
Vamos! *Let's go!*
Sempre foi a Portugal? *Did you go to Portugal (in the end/after all)?*

pôr

pôr a mesa *to set the table*
pôr de castigo *to punish*
Ela pô-lo na rua. *She turned him into the street (i.e. out of doors).*
pôr-se a *to begin to*
Ela pôs-se a falar muito depressa. *She began to speak hurriedly.*

O homem põe e Deus dispõe. *Man proposes and God disposes.*
sem tirar nem pôr *precisely/just like that*
o pôr do sol *sunset*

querer

se quiser *if you like*
como quiser (queira) *as you wish*
sem querer *unintentionally*
Ela fez por querer. *She did it on purpose.*
Queira sentar-se. *Please sit down.*
Quem quer vai, quem não quer manda. *If you want a thing done, do it yourself.*

ser

É isso mesmo. *That's just it.*
É sempre assim. *It always happens that way.*
Como foi que ...? *How did it happen that ...?*
É por minha conta. *It's on me.*
a não ser que *unless*
se eu fosse você ... *if I were you ...*
Seja como for ... *Be that as it may ...*
tal como deve ser *as it should be*
É a minha vez. *It is my turn.*
o ser humano *the human being*

ter

ter fome *to be hungry*
ter sêde *to be thirsty*
ter frio *to be cold*
ter calor *to be warm*
ter sono *to be sleepy*

ter razão *to be right*
ter pressa *to be in a hurry*
ter medo *to be afraid*
ter vinte anos *to be twenty years old*
ter saudades de *to feel longing, nostalgia for, to miss*
Que é que tem? *What is the matter with you?*
Tenho que terminar este trabalho. *I have to finish this work.*
Você tem de partir imediatamente. *You must leave immediately.*

Verbs requiring prepositions

The following verbs require a preposition before the infinitive of another verb:

acabar de *to finish (doing)*, *to have just (done)*
acabar por *to end up (doing)*
aconselhar a *to advise to*
ajudar a *to help to*
começar a *to begin to*
começar por *to begin by (doing)*
decidir-se a *to decide to*
lembrar-se de *to remember to*
obrigar a *to force*, *compel to*
pedir para *to ask to*
pensar em *to think of (doing)*
voltar a *(to do) again*
voltar para *to return to*

These verbs require a preposition before a noun or an infinitive:

acostumar-se a *to get used to*
acreditar em *to believe in*
aproximar-se de *to approach*
assistir a *to attend*
cansar-se de *to get tired of*
casar-se com *to get married to*
chegar a *to arrive at*
dar com *to come across*, *bump into*
dar para *to overlook*
dar por *to notice*
duvidar de *to doubt*
encontrar-se com *to meet (usually by arrangement)*
esquecer-se de *to forget*
gostar de *to like*
habituar-se a *to get used to*

ir a, ir para *to go to* (ir a *implies a shorter stay than* ir para)
olhar para *to look at*
parecer-se com *to look like, resemble*
pegar em *to pick up (in Brazil,* pegar *without preposition)*
precisar de *to need*
queixar-se de *to complain about*
reparar em *to notice*
sonhar com *to dream of*
sorrir para *to smile at*
vir a, vir para *to come to* (vir a *implies a shorter stay than* vir para)

Index of verbs

Abbreviations

DEF   defective, impersonal or unipersonal, see Part III, pp. 54-55
DPP   double past participle, see 'Tenses' in Part I, pp. 19-21
IRR   irregular. see list in Part III, pp. 62-81
O   orthographical-changing, see Part III, p. 61
RAD   radical-changing, see Part III, pp. 56-60
PP   irregular past participle, see 'Tenses' in Part I, p. 19
R   regular, see model conjugations in Part II, pp. 40-45
REF   reflexive, see model conjugations in Part II, pp. 46-51

aborrecer R *to bore*
  aborrecer-se (de) REF *to get bored (with)* 51
abrir PP *to open* 19
acabar R *to finish*
  acabar de *to have just* 87 (*see 'Auxiliaries'* 29), acabar por *to end up* 87
aceitar DPP *to accept* 19
acender DPP *to switch on* 19
aconselhar (a) R *to advise to* 87
acostumar-se a REF *to get used to* 51, 87
acreditar em R *to believe in* 87
acudir RAD (*like* subir) *to aid, go to the help of* 57
afligir DPP, O *to worry (someone)* 19, 61
  afligir-se REF, O *to get worried* 51, 61
agitar-se REF *to get excited, nervous, angry* 51
agradecer DPP *to thank* 19
agredir RAD *to assault, cause bodily harm* 57
ajudar (a) R *to help (to)* 87
alcançar O *to reach, achieve* 61
alugar O *to rent, let* 61
amar R *to love*
andar R *to be, move, walk* 40 (*see 'Auxiliaries'* 28)
anexar DPP *to annex* 19

ansiar RAD (*like* odiar) *to look forward to, yearn for* 59
aprender R *to learn*
apressar-se REF *to hurry* 51
approximar-se (de) REF *to approach* 51, 87
arranjar R *to get, obtain, repair, arrange*
   arranjar-se REF *to get ready (groom oneself), make do* 51
arrepender-se (de) REF *to repent, regret* 51
assistir a R *to attend* 87
banhar-se REF *to bathe oneself* 51
barbear RAD *to shave* 59
   barbear-se RAD, REF *to shave oneself* (*like* passear) 51, 59
benzer DPP *to bless* 19
bater R *to knock, beat*
beber R *to drink*
caber IRR *to fit in, be contained (in), have room* 62, 63, 65
cair RAD *to fall* 55
cansar R *to tire*
   cansar-se (de) REF *to get tired, tire (of)* 51, 87
casar-se (com) REF *to get married (to)* 51, 87
cativar DPP *to captivate* 19
cear RAD (*like* passear) *to have supper* 59
cegar DPP, O *to blind* 19, 61
chamar-se REF *to be called* 51
chegar (a) R *to arrive (at)* 87
chover DEF *to rain* 55
cobrir PP, RAD (*like* dormir) *to cover* 19, 58
começar (a/por) O *to begin (to/by)* 61, 87
comer R *to eat*
completar DPP *to complete* 19
concluir DPP *to conclude* (*like* diminuir) 19
conduzir RAD *to drive, conduct* 60
confundir DPP *to confound* 20
conhecer O *to know* 61
conseguir RAD, O *to achieve* (*like* seguir) 56
construir RAD (*like* subir) *to build* 57
consumir RAD *to consume* 57
convencer DPP, O *to convince* 20, 61

corromper DPP *to corrupt* 20

crer RAD *to believe* 59

cuspir RAD (*like* subir) *to spit* 58

dar IRR *to give* 62-64, 66 (*see 'Verbal idioms'* 82)

dar com/para/por IRR *to come across/overlook/notice* 87

decidir-se (a) REF *to decide (to)* 51, 87

defender DPP *to defend* 20

deitar R *to put (someone) to bed, pour (put in)*
   deitar-se REF *to lie down, go to bed* 51

deixar R *to let (allow), leave behind* (*see 'Verbal idioms* 82)

descalçar DPP, O *to take off (shoes)* 20, 61

descobrir RAD (*like* dormir) *to discover* 58

desertar DPP *to desert* 20

despedir-se REF, RAD (*like* pedir) *to take one's leave, say goodbye* 51, 59

despir RAD (*like* seguir) *to undress* 56
   despir-se REF, RAD *to get undressed* 51, 56

destruir RAD *to destroy* 58

dever R *to owe, ought* (*see 'Auxiliaries'* 25)

diminuir RAD *to lessen, diminish* 58

divertir RAD to amuse 56
   divertir-se REF, RAD *to enjoy oneself* 51, 56

dizer PP, IRR *to say, tell* 19, 62-64, 67

doer DEF, RAD *to hurt* (*like* moer) 55, 60

dormir RAD *to sleep* 58

duvidar de R *to doubt* 87

eleger DPP, O *to elect* 20, 61

emagrecer O *to lose weight* 61

embriagar-se REF *to get drunk* 51

encontrar R *to meet, find*
   encontrar-se (com) REF *to meet (someone)* 51, 87

enganar R *to deceive, cheat*
   enganar-se REF *to make a mistake* 51

engasgar-se REF, O *to choke* 51, 61

engolir RAD *to swallow* 58

entrar R *to enter, come in*

entregar (a) DPP, O *to deliver (to)* 20, 61
   entregar-se (a) REF, DPP, O *to surrender oneself (to)* 20, 51, 61

entusiasmar-se REF *to get enthusiastic, excited* 51
envolver DPP *to wrap, involve* 20
enxugar DPP, O *to dry* 20, 61
erigir DPP, O *to erect* 20, 61
escrever PP *to write* 19
esperar R *to wait, hope, expect*
esquecer-se (de) REF, O *to forget* 51, 61, 87
estar IRR *to be* 62-64, 68 (*see 'Auxiliaries'* 27 *and 'Verbal idioms'* 83)
estrear RAD (*like* passear) *to do for the first time* 59
exprimir DPP *to express* 20
expulsar DPP *to expel* 20
extinguir DPP, O *to extinguish* 20, 61
extrair DPP *to extract* 20
falar R *to speak* 40-45
falsificar DPP *to falsify* 20
fartar DPP *to have enough* 20
fazer PP, IRR *to do, make* 19, 62-64, 69 (*see 'Verbal idioms'* 83)
fechar R *to shut*
ferir RAD (*like* seguir) *to wound, hurt* 56
ficar O *to stay, be* 61 (*see 'Auxiliaries'* 29 *and 'Verbal idioms'* 84)
fingir R *to feign, pretend*
    fingir-se REF, O *to pretend to be* 51, 61
fixar DPP *to fix* 20
frigir DPP, O *to fry* 20, 61
fritar DPP *to fry* 20
fugir RAD, O *to run away, flee* 58, 61
fumar R *to smoke*
ganhar PP *to earn, win, gain* 19
gastar PP *to spend* 19
gostar de R *to like* 87
habituar-se (a) REF *to get used to* 51, 87
haver IRR *to have* 62-64, 70 (*see 'Auxiliaries'* 26, 29), DEF *there is/are* 55
importar-se REF *to mind, be concerned* 51
imprimir DPP *to print* 20
incendiar RAD (*like* odiar) *to set fire to* 59
incluir DPP *to include* (*like* diminuir) 20
infectar DPP *to infect* 20

inquietar DPP *to disturb, worry* 20

inserir DPP *to insert* 20

inverter DPP *to invert, reverse* 20

ir (a/para) IRR *to go (to)* 62-64, 71, 88 (*see 'Verbal idioms'* 84)

   ir-se embora IRR, REF *to go away* 51

isentar DPP *to exempt* 20

jazer DEF *to lie at rest* 54

jogar O *to play (games)* 61

juntar DPP *to join, gather in a pile, save (money)* 20

lamentar R *to regret, bewail*

   lamentar-se REF *to lament* 51

lavar R *to wash*

   lavar-se REF *to wash oneself, have a wash* 51

lembrar-se (de) REF *to remember* 51, 87

ler RAD *to read* 59

levantar-se REF *to get up* 51

libertar DPP *to free* 20

limpar DPP *to clean* 20

manifestar DPP *to manifest* 20

matar DPP *to kill* 20

medir RAD *to measure* 59

mentir RAD (*like* seguir) *to lie* 56

mexer-se REF *to move* 52

miar DEF *to mew* 55

moer RAD *to grind* 60

morrer DPP *to die* 20

mover-se REF *to move* 52

murchar DPP *to wilt, wither* 20

nadar R *to swim*

nascer O *to be born* 61

nevar DEF *to snow*

obrigar (a) O *to force, compel (to)* 61, 87

ocultar DPP *to hide* 20

odiar RAD *to hate* 58

olhar para R *to look at* 88

oprimir DPP *to oppress* 20

ouvir RAD *to hear, listen* 59

pagar PP, O *to pay* 19, 61

parecer O *to seem* 67

   parecer-se com REF, O *to look like, resemble* 52, 61, 88

partir R *to leave (depart), break* 40-45

passear RAD *to go for a walk* 59

pedir RAD *to ask for* 59 (pedir para *to ask to* 87)

pegar em O *to pick up* 61, 88

pensar (em) R *to think (of)* 87

pentear RAD (*like* passear) *to comb* 59

   pentear-se REF, RAD *to comb one's hair* 52, 59

perder RAD *to lose* 59

perseguir RAD, O *to pursue, harass* (*like* seguir) 56

perverter DPP *to prevent* 20

poder IRR *to be able* 62, 63, 72 (*see 'Auxiliaries'* 25)

pôr PP, IRR *to put, place* 19, 63, 64, 73 (*see 'Verbal idioms'* 84)

possuir RAD *to possess, own* (*like* diminuir)

prazer DEF *to please* 54

precisar de R *to need* 88

preferir RAD (*like* seguir) *to prefer* 56

prender DPP *to arrest, imprison* 21

preocupar-se REF *to worry, be preoccupied* 52

prevenir RAD (*like* agredir) *to warn* 57

professar DPP *to profess* 21

progredir RAD (*like* agredir) *to progress, advance* 57

queixar-se (de) REF *to complain about* 52, 88

querer IRR *to want* 63, 64, 74 (*see 'Verbal idioms'* 85)

reaver DEF *to have again* 54

recear RAD (*like* passear) *to fear* 59

recusar-se (a) REF *to refuse (to)* 52

reflectir RAD *to reflect* 56

remediar RAD *to rectify, remedy* 59

   remediar-se REF, RAD *to make do* 52, 59

remir RAD *to redeem* 60

reparar R *to repair*

   reparar em R *to notice* 88

repelir DPP *to repel* 21

repetir RAD (*like* seguir) *to repeat* 56

respeitar R *to respect*

restringir DPP, O *to restrain* 21, 61

revolver DPP *to revolve* 21

rir IRR *to laugh* 63, 75

   rir-se de REF, IRR *to make fun of, laugh at* 52, 63, 75

roer RAD *to gnaw* 60

romper DPP *to break, tear* 21

saber IRR *to know* 62-64, 76 (*see 'Auxiliaries'* 25)

sacudir RAD (*like* fugir) *to shake off* 58

sair RAD (*like* cair) *to go out* 58

salvar DPP *to save, salvage* 21

secar DPP *to dry* 21

seguir RAD, O *to follow* 56, 61

segurar DPP *to hold* 21

sentar-se REF *to sit down* 46-50

sentir RAD *to feel* 57

   sentir-se REF, RAD *to feel (well, ill, happy, etc.)* 52, 57

ser IRR *to be* 62-64, 77 (*see 'Auxiliaries'* 27 and 'Verbal idioms' 85)

servir RAD *to serve, be good for* 57

   servir-se (de) REF, RAD *to help oneself (to), make use (of)* 52, 57

soar RAD *to sound* 60

soltar DPP *to loosen* 21

sonhar com R *to dream of* 88

sorrir (para) IRR (*like* rir) *to smile (at)* 63, 75, 88

subir RAD *to go up* 57

submergir O, DPP *to submerge* 21

submeter DPP *to submit* 21

   submeter-se DPP, REF *to submit oneself* 21, 52

sujeitar DPP *to subdue, subject*

   sujeitar-se DPP, REF *to subject oneself* 21, 52

sumir-se REF, RAD *to vanish* 52, 58

suspeitar DPP *to suspect* 21

suspender DPP *to suspend* 21

telefonar R *to telephone*

ter IRR *to have* 62-64, 78 (*see 'Auxiliaries'* 26, 29 and 'Verbal idioms' 85)

terminar R *to end, finish, terminate*

tingir DPP, O *to dye, tinge* 21, 61

tirar R *to take off (remove), take out from*
tornar R *to turn* (tornar a *to do again, see 'Auxiliaries'* 29)
tossir RAD (*like* dormir) *to cough* 58
trabalhar R *to work*
transferir RAD (*like* seguir) *to transfer* 57
transgredir RAD (*like* agredir) *to infringe, transgress* 57
tratar R *to treat*
   tratar-se de REF, DEF *to be about, concern (something)* 52, 55
trazer IRR *to bring* 62-64, 79
uivar DEF *to howl* 55
valer RAD *to be worth* 59
vender R *to sell* 40-45
ver PP, IRR *to see* 19, 63, 80
vestir RAD *to dress* 57
   vestir-se REF, RAD *to get dressed* 52, 57
vir (a/para) PP, IRR *to come (to)* 19, 62-64, 81, 88
voar RAD *to fly* 60
voltar R *to turn, return*
   voltar a *to do again* 87 (*see 'Auxiliaries'* 29), voltar para *to return to* 87
zangar-se REF *to be angry* 52